Don't Call Me a Drama Queen!

Don't Call Me a Drama Queen!

*A Guide for the Overly Sensitive
and Their Significant Others Who Need
to Lighten Up and Go with the Flow*

DR. DEBRA MANDEL

alyson books
NEW YORK

In order to protect the anonymity and privacy of my clients, I've changed names, circumstances, and other identifying information. In some cases, I've created composites that closely resemble the experiences of real people. Any similarity to actual people is coincidental. The information in the book is meant to educate, illustrate, and inspire people who struggle with the drama queen syndrome and their significant others. The content is in no way intended to be a replacement for professional help.

Manufactured in the United States of America

A trade paperback original published by Alyson Books
245 West 17th Street, New York, NY 10011

Distribution in the United Kingdom by Turnaround Publisher Services Ltd.
Unit 3, Olympia Trading Estate, Coburg Road, Wood Green
London N22 6TZ England

First Edition: October 2008

08 09 10 11 12 13 14 15 16 17 a 10 9 8 7 6 5 4 3 2 1

ISBN-10: 1593501013
ISBN-13: 978-1593501013

Library of Congress Cataloging-in-Publication data are on file.
Cover design by Victor Mingovits
Interior design by Elliott Beard

I dedicate this book to all the lovable drama queens and their significant others who have shared their stories with me and who have allowed me to help guide them onto a path of tranquility and happiness. Please always remember that your sensitivity is a gift; it just needs to be channeled in a more nurturing and constructive way. Thank you for trusting me to help you with your healing. No doubt, your stories will serve as an inspiration for other lovable queens to begin their journey toward hope and peace of mind.

—Hugs, Dr. Debra

Contents

Acknowledgments

Thanks to all of my friends for your never-ending support, love, and encouragement. I hope you all know who you are and how much I appreciate how you have stood by me through thick and thin! And special thanks to Michael who has been through more ups and downs with me than anyone in my whole life. And to Tom, a new friend, who has gone above and beyond the call of duty to help me continue to enhance my media career.

Thanks to Linda Konner, my literary agent. There are no words to describe how important your role has been in my life. It's hard to believe that this is our third book together. Were it not for you, I probably would have thrown in the towel after our first. But through your continued encouragement and trust in my ability to come up with new and fresh ideas, you've given me the confidence to keep on writing. I especially thank you for your constructive criticism and for always pushing me to become a better writer. You're the best.

Thanks to Richard Fumosa and Anthony La Sasso and the rest of the gang at Alyson. Your excitement and enthusiasm for this book gives me hope and inspiration to make this a number one bestseller.

Acknowledgments

Thanks to Mindy and Herbert, the production team for my new television show. You both make me feel like a star.

Thanks to Cheryl, my sister, Dora, my stepmom, and my dearest dad, for never giving up on me throughout all our family's trials and tribulations. Your support means the world to me. And, Dad, I'll always have a smile on my face when I think about the cute little phrases you coined to teach me life's lessons—my favorite, of course, "Love is not a potato."

Thanks to my deceased mom. If you were still here, I'd give you a big hug and let you know that I love you, despite all the issues we were never able to work out. And my life would not be complete were it not for the special children in my life: Remi, Delainey, and Rachel. I hope you girls know how special you are and that your lives flourish with love and happiness.

Special, special thanks to Tiffany, my daughter, and my breath of fresh air. Who would ever think that a teenage girl would be, at times, a better role model of emotional stability than her own mother? Tiffany, you always teach me wonderful lessons about what's really important in life. You inspired this book when you one day said to me, so matter-of-factly, "Mom, if it's not going to bother me six months from now, why let it bother me now?" You're brilliant and I love you!

Last, but not least, thanks to my beloved, Chris. You give me new hope every day for long-lasting love. Thanks for laughing and crying with me and never judging me harshly. You're a great man.

Don't Call Me a Drama Queen!

Introduction

No matter how diligent we are in our quests for happiness, we find that life inevitably tosses us many unavoidable curve balls—often ones we'd rather do without. Yet most of these unpleasant events and experiences don't *have* to cause undue stress, anger, or any other form of unrest. For instance, the mother of a child who constantly throws temper tantrums doesn't have to become upset every time one happens. The wife whose husband fails to clean up after himself doesn't have to pull out her hair in frustration. And the homeowner whose power gets turned off because he forgot to pay the electric bill doesn't have to feel ashamed or perceive the world as cruel.

Granted, such situations may cause some people to go into a tizzy, but this doesn't have to be the case. Why? Because whether we're aware of it or not, we can minimize stress and profoundly increase peace and joy in our lives once we fully embrace our power to *choose* how we respond to the ups and down of day-to-day living. And while this may seem like a simple enough formula on paper, far too many of us can't put it into practice because we don't believe we can actually make conscious decisions about how we feel and how we react. Hence, many people react to life like a knee jerking in response to a doctor checking for reflexes.

I'm not saying that we can avoid all unpleasantness. There are certainly situations that would typically produce strong negative emotions, terror, or extreme stress in everyone—witnessing a plane crash, being trapped in a burning building, or getting held up at gunpoint. But how often do we encounter such traumas or potentially life-threatening moments in our *daily* lives? For most of us, the answer is "not too often, if ever." Yet millions of us walk the planet in a perpetual state of distress, suffering from conditions ranging all the way from mild anxiety to suicidal depression. Some people feel exasperated all the time, even when their lives are fairly peaceful. And we all know how damaging chronic stress can be to our bodies, often leading to life-threatening conditions, such as heart attacks, hypertension, strokes, cancer, diabetes, and cancer (visit www.HELPGUIDE.org for a comprehensive explanation of the effects of stress).

While some over-reactors truly do suffer from actual mental or medical conditions requiring professional help, most are simply trapped in what I call the *drama queen syndrome*. This doesn't mean that such people mean to be so hypersensitive or overly reactive to each subtle nuance of life—they just can't seem to help themselves, or so they believe.

Contrary to what the media portrays, drama queens aren't always stereotypical. They come from all walks of life, regardless of age, gender, race, sexual orientation, or socioeconomic status.

As a drama queen you perceive danger when there is none. You personalize things that aren't personal. You spend hours a day trying to control things you have no control over. You fear you won't receive your fair share of things, often feeling mistreated or put upon by others. You're usually very sensitive to changes in your routines and you may become quickly overwhelmed by even mild stimuli. You commonly take on far too much burden of responsibility for other people's happiness while si-

Introduction

multaneously storing resentments for carrying too much unnecessary weight on your own shoulders. You're often easily offended.

As a drama queen, you feel like you're constantly on the receiving end of a boxer's left hook. Yet once you're more removed from the situation you originally reacted to, you almost always feel foolish for having made such a big deal out of what turned out to be nothing. But you can't seem to break the cycle. Sadly, you may destroy your loving relationships because you constantly need to receive comforting and soothing.

While some drama queens resemble "emotional vampires," that is, people who suck others dry, give nothing back, and really don't give a damn about the impact of their behavior on others, most usually have had good reasons for having developed an over-reactive style because, at some point, they actually were in powerless positions without choices. Sadly, however, they don't recognize that danger no longer exists. Hence they don't believe they can truly lighten up.

Sounds grim, doesn't it? Don't despair. If this describes you or someone you know and love, you're already well on your way to learning how to cruise through stress simply by having picked up this book. With this book you'll learn how to:

- say "good-bye" once and for all to unnecessary response styles that cause you to feel unhappy, angry, resentful, disappointed, and stressed-out by daily life
- distinguish potentially traumatic, life-threatening, or truly dangerous situations which warrant an exaggerated response from those that aren't a huge deal by using the R.E.A.C.T. guide (Reality, Emergency, Action, Consequence, and Thought)
- become comfortable letting go of the need to control situations, people, and places
- focus on the present moment

- transform negative situations into true positives
- learn to accept life on all of its terms

During my twenty-plus years as a psychologist and working with lov-able drama queens (including myself), I've witnessed hundreds of trans-formations. Using the methods outlined in the book, even people who've endured some of the most heinous traumas imaginable have been able to leave their experiences in the past and enjoy their lives fully in the pres-ent. Using a compassionate, yet no-nonsense approach, this book is filled with checklists, exercises, and real-life examples, making the methods and tools simple and easy to incorporate into your life.

This book reassures you that your body's innate survival instincts, which allow you to fight, take flight, or freeze when faced with true danger, will remain intact, as will your ability to experience intense feelings. After all, sometimes getting irritated and making a lot of noise makes sense. But, more often than not, intense reactions aren't necessary or in service of our needs. For instance, perfectionism may be a great asset for a brain surgeon in the middle of removing a frontal-lobe tumor, but a characteristic such as this becomes a liability if you're trying to enjoy a picnic on the beach with a loved one. Similarly, the ability to react quickly and intensely may actually prove to be very useful in a real crisis such as during a bank robbery—but such a high-level response won't serve you very well when buying a pair of shoes. This book describes when such reactions are warranted and when they're inappropriate and/ or self-destructive.

Certainly there are countless resources available that teach the art of stress management, anger reduction, and how to lead happier lives. But for drama queens, these tools either fail entirely or remain Band-Aids. Not because of a lack of intelligence, but because drama queens can't incorporate these other methods of soothing. They lack the foundation for understanding *why* they have such strong reactions to begin with, and they are missing the *tools* to make positive changes. Plus, they don't believe that they will be okay if they let down their guard and stop worrying so much. So they can't incorporate the methods in a meaningful way. *Don't Call Me a Drama Queen!* takes a huge leap beyond the other resources by teaching the art of stress *prevention*.

If what I'm describing applies to you, but you're a bit tentative to accept the label of "drama queen," please don't disregard this information prematurely. You're not alone in this category and there's nothing to be ashamed of. This book isn't addressed to the "emotional vampires" whom we commonly confuse with drama queens (more on this distinction later). You *are* among many millions of people, old and young, single and attached, of higher education or not, who are sick and tired of being referred to as a "drama queen." You've probably been repeatedly told by others to "stop making mountains out of molehills" and you're tired of being labeled and judged. Or, maybe you're in a relationship with someone you believe is a drama queen (your brother, your mother, your lover, or best friend) and you're frustrated with the ups and downs. You've often thought about dumping the relationship but you're hoping there's a way you can become more helpful and possibly improve the connection.

People commonly misunderstand drama queens, believing that they are trying to cause trouble. And while drama queens may enjoy the upside of their dramatics, such as when other people find them amusing and fun to be around, they can certainly do without the downside. But they just don't know how else to be, since they don't recognize that their reactions are of their own choosing. *Don't Call Me a Drama Queen!* will help de-stigmatize this label and give you a new perspective so you can regain a sense of humor about life. This book is definitely for you if:

- You're tired of being a ping-pong ball in a never-ending game of life.

- You feel helpless but want to take charge of your reactions, once and for all.
- You have been unsuccessful at stress management and you understand you have a deeper problem that you need to address.
- Your doctor or loved ones have pleaded with you to take it easier and learn to chill out.
- Your physical health has become compromised.
- You feel easily defeated, irritated, anxious, upset, disappointed, or any other unpleasant emotion.
- You worry a lot and have trouble taking constructive action.
- You experience high levels of stress, even when life is generally going well.
- You desire a happier, more tranquil state of mind.

If you don't relate to these descriptions, you will still benefit from reading this book. Everyone knows at least one person in his/her inner circle who suffers from the drama queen syndrome. And while you may be at your wit's end in terms of dealing with this person in a relationship, you probably care deeply for him or her and don't necessarily want to throw in the towel if you can help it. In fact, the more that those who are close to the drama queen understand the condition, the less likely it is that they will get annoyed with the one who appears to be in a perpetual state of hysteria.

Now let's get down to the nitty-gritties. Let's find out at what level you or your loved one rate on the drama queen scale and begin to work your way toward positive solutions.

Special note: If you've read any of my other books, you understand that I'm all about love and acceptance. Healing whatever we have to heal should be within the context of warmth and kindness. While I can be very direct and say it like it is, my tone can also be playful and my intention is to encourage honest assessment. Being a drama queen does not mean you're a bad person in any way. We're all screwed up in some way or another and it is our hardships and adversities that bring strength to our character.

All I ask is that you read on with an open mind and a curiosity to discover things about yourself. You're hurting on some level or most likely you wouldn't have been drawn to this book. Denial is the worst condition of all because it prohibits growth and change. Please allow yourself to take in whatever descriptions or advice seems useful. Many of the things I say or suggest may not apply to you—but give yourself a chance to take in a little. Maybe you'll be surprised.

PART I

The Problem

Chapter 1

Are You a Drama Queen?
—Take the Test

We're all familiar with the classic stereotype of a drama queen—those gals and guys who make large "flamboyant" gestures, speak with a high-pitched voice, and react to everything in a much bigger way than anyone else around them. Not only do they embellish life's tough stuff, they also exaggerate the good things. Their ups are higher than Mt. Whitney and their downs are lower than the bottom of the Atlantic Ocean, even though many continue to lead functional lives. For the most part, they don't suffer from any clinically diagnosable mental or physical condition.

Yet drama queens have so much more depth to them than the stereotypical description above. And sadly, they tend to be chronically misunderstood. Contrary to popular belief, they don't intend to harm others. In fact, they usually recognize their tendency to overreact and want to change. But they simply don't know how. Drama queens don't need to be shamed or ridiculed or told they "make mountains out of molehills." Rather, they desperately need tender loving care, accompanied by a prescriptive guide for how to soothe and contain the underlying triggers of their emotional roller-coaster rides. Then, they can finally experience a new, more effective, way of approaching the world.

Just in case you're feeling any shame or reluctance to embrace the concept that you might be a drama queen—especially since the label often carries a negative image—please note the following very important distinction. When I refer to drama queens, I'm not talking about those people who are better termed "emotional vampires"—that is, people who don't give a rat's ass about others, who don't experience any particular distress over the dramatic way they react to the world and the people they encounter, and who would have us believe their lives would be ruined if there were no more Prada bags or Seven jeans.

Unlike the drama queens I refer to throughout this book, emotional vampires suck the energy from everyone else and give nothing back. They have superficial relationships, at best, and they are permanently committed to seeing themselves as victimized by the world because they have no sense of personal responsibility for their actions. They rarely see their behavior as problematic in any way. Many even truly believe they're entitled to wreak havoc on the lives of their significant others (or even strangers for that matter), and they have a general disregard for the rights of others. True, emotional vampires can be quite comical and entertaining at times, particularly while viewing them on the big screen. But in real life, they rarely change their behavior, let alone seek help, and they can ultimately be very toxic.

Given that you picked up this book, you've already failed to meet the criteria for an emotional vampire. So toss that image right out of your head. I trust that at least on some level you recognize you have a tendency to overreact and you want to make positive changes. And as I'm sure you're already well aware, the only way to fix a problem and improve your life is to acknowledge that you have a problem. I know it can be very difficult to admit to having emotional issues, especially if you feel ashamed about them. So please be assured that there is nothing wrong with you if you fit the description of a drama queen. There are good reasons why you and other people become hyper-reactive and you will soon learn about the causes of the drama queen syndrome. So please toss aside any negative connotations and read ahead with an open mind and a willingness to assess your behavior honestly.

Characteristics and Consequences of Being a Drama Queen: Is This You or Someone You Love?

As I've already mentioned, drama queens come from all walks of life and in many different packages. But despite these outward differences, they share many underlying commonalities. They are often highly intelligent, sensitive (too sensitive, in fact), and compassionate. They often care too much about others, worrying endlessly about the potential dangers that could befall their loved ones.

These people aren't the same as the selfish, attention-seeking emotional vampires I described earlier. Granted, drama queens often command more attention than the average person, but not because they consciously wish to drive people crazy. Rather, most drama queens I've worked with behave as they do because they don't know of a better way to behave and they truly believe their reactions are necessary and fully warranted in the moment. Without knowing why or how to be different, these people chronically react to life as if in a state of crisis almost all of the time. Yet beneath their seemingly ridiculous reactions, there usually lies a very frightened being—someone who believes catastrophe can and will strike at any moment.

Drama queens know they react more intensely than a situation requires but they can't seem to stop themselves. They've been told repeatedly that they make big deals out of nothing and they frequently get teased for being so reactive. Not surprisingly, they often suffer from a fragile self-image and low self-esteem.

The Problem

Some are so reactive to life's stimuli that they become exhausted to the point where they may even have trouble getting out of bed in the morning. But don't get me wrong. Most drama queens often do lead functional lives—they hold down jobs and raise responsible kids—although they often become exhausted to the point where they may even have trouble getting out of bed in the morning. But even for those who seem to function well, it's not without tremendous consequences to their happiness. In fact, the life of a drama queen can be highly tumultuous, physically taxing, and extremely unpleasant. Believe me, I know this first-hand—both from having been a full-blown drama queen myself—and from having worked with hundreds of drama queens.

Though drama queens have little, if any, awareness of their hyper-reactivity while in the midst of a situation, once the dust has settled, they often smack themselves on the forehead and ponder in disgust, "Why did I let that get to me so much?" Or, they think, "What in the world came over me? Other people didn't even think twice about what I freaked out about." Once they come to recognize that they've unnecessarily exploded, they frequently become remorseful about the emotional messes they've created. To assuage their guilt, they work overtime to clean up the fallout from their hysterics, forever apologizing to their spouses, friends, coworkers, bosses, and children for having made such a big deal out of nothing. But they lose credibility. Without an understanding of why they react as they do—and the knowledge that they have the power to choose different reactions—drama queens inevitably respond with the same habitual reactivity the next time they hit a bump in the road.

Sadly, drama queens have received a horrible rap, which in turn makes it very hard for them to seek help or even recognize that they have a problem. They're frequently the target of many cruel jokes, often referred to in condescending and degrading terms. What most people fail to realize is that even though drama queens have a strong desire to mellow out, they don't trust that they will be safe if they let go of their intense reactions.

Are You a Drama Queen?—Take the Test

Because of the confusion about drama queens, many people misperceive them as being stuck-up or as flaunting an air of superiority. And rightfully so. Let's face the facts, drama queens: we can be very demanding and difficult to be around. "Why is she getting so riled up about nothing?" would be a common reaction from an onlooker witnessing a drama queen in action. To the normal reactor, the drama queen's response seems odd. But to the drama queen, there is no other acceptable reaction. What most fail to realize is that the drama queen has good intentions behind his/her exaggerated responses.

Drama queens often have nowhere to turn for help. They become quickly stigmatized as someone who makes things up, like the boy in the fable *The Boy Who Cried Wolf.* Should a drama queen report an actual danger, it's likely that no one will take him or her seriously because he or she's already blasted too many false alarms.

Chronically reacting to life as though it serves up danger isn't the only thing that causes trouble. Drama queens can also become very uncomfortable during peaceful or tranquil moments, perceiving that these are mere lulls before the inevitable storms. So even if there's nothing objective to worry about, the drama queen will find a reason to freak out. Oftentimes they're simply reacting as if they are still a child in a helpless position. It should come as no surprise then that drama queens have serious trouble kicking back and relaxing.

Diana, a thirty-five-year-old mother of two, had been raised in a family with high conflict. Her mom and dad were constantly at war with one another, and Diana realized early on that the only way she would possibly be noticed by her parents was to exaggerate everything. She also lived in a constant state of fear that her parents would divorce and that she would become the target of their frustration. She developed a very keen sense about the emotional climate in the family, and she usually felt as though she was walking on eggshells. She would bottle up her feelings and then inevitably explode at an inappropriate time. For instance, if she misspelled a word on a pop quiz in English class she might go off the deep end, even though she had maintained a solid A.

As Diana matured, she carried over into adulthood the coping style she'd learned in childhood. She had a difficult time relaxing and staying in the moment. She continually found herself worrying about things going wrong and she couldn't trust that good things would happen to her. If a friend failed to return her phone call, she'd panic and think the friend had been in a horrible accident. Or, she would convince herself that she must have done something terribly offensive to make her friend never want to speak to her again. Of course, when her friend finally called to say "hi," with nothing having happened other than the fact that she'd been busy, Diana would feel embarrassed for having blown things out of proportion.

Diana's dramatics interfered with all of her relationships. Though people initially found her to be very personable and likeable, she sabotaged a number of connections because, over time, others would often come to perceive her as being too high-maintenance. After a while, her apologies didn't hold any weight—when the next minor shake-up would occur, she'd again have a reflexively strong reaction of fear, upset, hurt, or sadness. Sometimes she would even become enraged for no good reason and she feared she might someday react with violence.

Like many drama queens, Diana's intense reactions also had positive elements. Having learned how to entertain people and make them laugh through exaggerated acts of silliness, she could resurrect even the most boring of all parties or coax a smile from even the unhappiest of children. As long as she wasn't in the middle of a drama reaction, she could also be quite demonstrative in her affection—a quality her children truly cherished. But sadly, she would quickly shift from happy-go-lucky into drama queen mode in a split second if *she* perceived a potential crisis or danger. For instance, if one person out of twenty failed to laugh at one of her improvisations, she could plummet into despair, believing that she'd ruined the evening. Or, if one of her children stubbed a toe, she'd be ready to call 911.

Are You a Drama Queen?—Take the Test

Diana hadn't realized just how many unresolved issues she had carried over from her childhood into her adulthood until the day she freaked out while dropping off her eleven-year-old daughter, Tracey, at school. They were ten minutes late—generally not something that most people would consider to be a crisis. Yet sadly for both of them, Diana reacted as though her daughter was about to be expelled from school for selling cocaine. Seeing her mom rapidly spiraling into a frenzy, Tracey matter-of-factly said, "Mom, chill out—it's not a big deal if I'm tardy once in a while. I'm only in sixth grade!" At that moment, Diana realized her daughter was more grounded and stable than she was. And she realized she had better end this cycle once and for all. She certainly didn't want to have her kids feel the same instability she had felt while growing up.

Amanda, a twenty-two-year-old college student, also developed the drama queen syndrome. Unlike Diana, however, who never had her fear come true—that her parents would divorce—one of Amanda's worst fears from childhood was realized when she was about twelve. And tragically, she was left to cope with no guidance.

Amanda had been given a small dog named Cuddles that she completely adored. She and Cuddles were inseparable. And as is common for children, she loved him so much that she often worried about losing him to some unforeseeable circumstance. Her fears would range from, "What if Cuddles runs away and never comes back?" to "Cuddles might get sick and die and then what will I do?" Sometimes the potential loss of Cuddles was all she could think about. Wouldn't you know it: one day while she was sitting on her front porch doing her homework, Cuddles bolted out into the street chasing a ball, got hit by a car, and died almost instantly.

Amanda was devastated and she had held herself responsible for all these years. (I still get a tear in my eye when I reflect on this story she told.) Amanda's parents felt really bad for her loss. But they weren't very good at soothing her or helping her with her grief—actually that's putting it mildly. In reality, they were completely inept at providing any comfort at all and Amanda was left feeling as though she was a horrible person. Amanda blamed herself for having not watched Cuddles more closely and she wouldn't forgive herself. She ended up developing a very strong belief that she must constantly be vigilant to danger and must personally protect everyone and everything she loves. Her fear of loss became so strong that she was looking over her shoulder for danger around the clock.

Amanda couldn't sustain an intimate relationship because whenever there was the slightest bit of trouble with a beau, she'd go into an emotional tizzy. The intensity of her reactions overwhelmed others. A guy would say, "Hey, relax, we'll get through this." But she would quickly turn a small problem into a disaster and then worry that she'd be abandoned. And then before you know it, the guy would end up breaking up with her. She projected so much tragedy onto even completely benign situations that eventually she created a self-fulfilling prophecy.

Thankfully, Amanda sought help. And by making the link between old unresolved hurts from her childhood and her current drama queen reactions, Amanda was able to begin the journey of taming her responses when faced with minor inconveniences and irritations of life. And she learned to distinguish perceived danger from real crises.

Common Myths

While the emotional vampires described earlier don't give a rat's ass about what other people think about them, this description would hardly do justice to the very large population of people whose dramatics cause them severe distress and who truly wish they could stop overreacting. Sadly, many drama queens make repeated visits to physicians and psychiatrists, desperately seeking a miracle chill pill. Yet while some drama queens do actually suffer from biochemical or hormonal abnormalities requiring medication or a serious psychological condition—such as post-traumatic stress disorder, major depression, or panic disorder—millions of people who meet the criteria for being a drama queen don't need a pill at all, and they most likely don't suffer from a serious mental condition. Rather, they need an attitude overhaul so they can come to recognize that they no longer have to be a slave to their emotional reactions. They simply need to learn a new way of responding to life's curve balls.

Please note that if you fear you or your loved one may be suffering from a clinically diagnosable condition, refer to the last chapter of this book for more clarification and professional resources.

Below are some of the common myths people hold about drama queens. Even drama queens themselves often buy into these misconceptions. Yet in my over two decades of experience, these are not the realities of people who suffer from drama queen syndrome. And these myths need to be dispelled once and for all. Among the most common myths drama queens:

- consciously choose to overreact because it makes them feel good
- are attention hogs
- have nothing better to do than stir up the pot
- enjoy making other people tense or nervous
- choose this way of being
- don't suffer as a result of their over-reactivity
- have no good reason for their behavior
- are emotionally immature

If you're anything like who I was when my drama queen syndrome was in full swing, you're tired of these stigmas and you wish people would be able to truly understand your suffering. And if you're a significant other of a drama queen, you need a different framework for understanding your loved one so that you will no longer get so exasperated by his/her responses.

The Problem

Myth Busters

A better description of a drama queen includes the following character-istics. Drama queens:

- don't know how to manage their intense reactions
- give too much power to their emotions because they don't know or trust that there is another way
- don't know how to constructively channel their sensitivities
- feel easily overwhelmed, even by seemingly benign stimuli
- have strong fears that bad things will happen, believing that by being hyper-vigilant they can prevent tragedies
- can and do change if given the proper tools

The Test

Now that you have a clearer idea of what a drama queen is/isn't, please take the test and see where you fall on the continuum. Keep in mind that this is a simple, unscientific assessment I've put together after years of working with drama queens, myself included. This tool has not been empirically validated. It's just meant to be a guide to help you get an idea of your own drama queen potential.

You may not identify with any of the items, yet still believe that you are a drama queen in need of assistance. Or you may see yourself in all of these items, yet not identify at all with what I'm describing. But assuming that you picked up this book because it spoke to you in some way, either concerning yourself or a significant other, you'll probably identify with some of the statements listed. If you do find that you relate to many or even all of the items, don't become hopeless or helpless. You're in good company and you can greatly increase your happiness and contentment by employing the tools outlined in the chapters ahead.

Are You a Drama Queen?—Take the Test

So dive in, be as honest and reflective as you can, and rate the following twenty-five items using the scale below:

Never (0)
Rarely (1)
Sometimes (2)
Frequently (3)
Always (4)

1. I easily and quickly get upset over minor events.
2. I don't recognize the intensity of my reaction while it's happening.
3. I feel like my body and emotions have a life of their own.
4. I can't seem to stop myself from overreacting even when I'm aware that I'm being too intense.
5. Other people have told me that I make mountains out of molehills (or something to that effect), implying that I tend to be overly sensitive.
6. I've had some childhood traumas or dramas that left me fearful that bad things would happen if I were to stop being vigilant.
7. I have trouble trusting that things will turn out okay.
8. I try to control things I really don't have any control over like how other people will react or behave.
9. I have a hard time relaxing in the moment when there is no apparent danger or imminent need to worry about anything.
10. I worry about the health and well-being of the people I'm close to, seemingly more than other people do.
11. I act in overprotective ways toward the people I care about—I give them warnings about things to worry about or feel compelled to alert them of what could go wrong if they take any risks at all.
12. I have trouble trusting my own ability to handle situations when something goes wrong.
13. I'm edgy during leisure time.

14. I tend to perceive danger even when there isn't any.

15. I regret having reacted to things with such intensity.

16. I have mood swings not attributable to any biochemical or hormonal cause and I can shift from super-happy to super-sad in a split second, simply because of a minor change in my surroundings.

17. I get stuck thinking about the worst possible consequence of a situation rather than focusing on the potential positive outcome.

18. I take life too seriously.

19. I react very strongly to other people's criticisms and disappointments in me and have a hard time shaking them off, even when I disagree with their assessment.

20. I have a strong need for approval from others, even from people who are insignificant in my life.

21. I complicate simple situations by worrying about things I have no control over.

22. Sometimes my friends or family members don't tell me things right away because they believe I will get too upset.

23. I feel jealous or envious when other people get more attention than I'm getting, even though I don't really want to steal the attention away from them.

24. I fear that my life isn't as important as other people's and sometimes feel I need to exaggerate the good or bad stuff so people will notice me.

25. I have a hard time accepting rejection.

Now tally up your score. I also suggest that you re-take the test and answer it from the perspective of a significant friend or loved one describing you. In other words, how would someone else rate you on these items if he or she were answering on your behalf? Or you might actually ask a trusted friend or loved one to take this test, keeping you in mind and then compare his/her results to your own self-appraisal. After all, sometimes other people can see us far more clearly than we can see ourselves.

Next, refer to the evaluation below to see where you fall on the drama queen continuum. But remember, this is not rocket science. And you should most definitely also seek a medical and/or psychological evaluation if you strongly agree with several of the items listed and/or if your life feels out of control. You may very well be suffering from a biochemical and/or psychological condition requiring professional help (more in-depth coverage on this is in Chapter Ten).

Score: 0–5

If you scored in this range, you probably won't benefit too much from the tools in this book since you don't even remotely resemble a drama queen. However, it's possible that you find the thought of being considered a drama queen to be shameful or embarrassing. Hence, you may not have been able to answer honestly since you may not yet be ready to acknowledge your drama queen potential. If that's the case, then I hope you will continue reading anyway and maybe you'll find some useful pearls along the way. Or maybe you truly don't suffer at all from this syndrome but you may find helpful information for someone you know who does, in fact, fit the description.

Score 6–25: Level One

If you scored in this range, you probably suffer only some minor traces of being a drama queen. This would be a fairly common scoring range for people who really wouldn't consider their style of reacting to be of any cause for concern. If you have once considered yourself a drama queen or people have described you as such, then you may have already had some therapy or self-help for this very issue and have resolved your tendency toward overreacting. Three cheers for you! Or you may be someone who has been fortunate enough to have been born with an easygoing temperament and who grew up in a nurturing environment that supported your at-ease style. So maybe on occasion you tend to overreact, but hey who doesn't? Nevertheless while this probably doesn't affect your functioning or the quality of your relationships in any significant way, you may very well find an exercise, suggestion, or new tool in this book to help you learn to enjoy life even more than you already do.

If you believe you are struggling with the consequences of being a drama queen but you still scored in this range, don't worry. The items included in the assessment simply may not adequately reflect how the drama queen in you manifests herself. For instance, you may experience high levels of anxiety most of the day and that's all you're aware of so you may not identify with many of the items. Yet you still believe it's because you overreact to things. No problem. Remember this assessment is simply an awareness tool. You know what you're dealing with, so if you relate to the other descriptions, you can most definitely benefit from the information that follows.

Score 26–50: Level Two

If you scored in this range you may experience either an ongoing low-level of distress or you have periodic flare-ups of considerable distress. You may be fine when your environment is very peaceful and predictable, but may unravel when there's an unforeseen change in your daily structure or routine. When these minor setbacks occur you might notice that it's hard to continue to go with the flow and take life on its own terms. For instance, you might feel great when you manage to leave for work on time, the traffic moves at a steady pace, *and* your boss shows up to the office in a good mood. But should there be a hiccup in any of these things—you get a flat tire, or get get stuck on the phone with your nagging mother, which then makes you late to the office—you become frazzled. For an easygoing, non-drama-queen-type of person, none of these events would be a big deal. Rather, they would just be blips in the road of life. But to the drama queen, these can be very upsetting.

If you scored in this range, you might be surprised that you qualify as a drama queen, especially if your picture of a drama queen resembles one of the stereotypes I mentioned earlier. But remember, drama queens come in many varieties. They're not just hysterical, overindulged performing artists or trust-fund brats. (I'm sure you can think of a few of these in the entertainment world—but I won't mention names.) They can also be highly productive, lovable, and endearing. And while you may not see your reactivity as having consequences that warrant the need to make any changes, believe it or not, you can make your life significantly more enjoyable and tranquil with just a few tweaks to how you perceive the world. So I highly recommend you keep reading and practice the exercises so you can reap even greater rewards in life. Why settle for "okay" when you can have "awesome"?

Score 51–75: Level Three

If you scored in this range, you most likely have a keen awareness of your tendency to overreact. You've probably often been told something akin to "you're too sensitive" or "you make big deals out of nothing." You may have heard more times than you'd like that you should just "chill-out," "lighten up," or "relax." (I've certainly been given these types of directives from significant others more than a time or two in the past.) You likely have a difficult time enjoying yourself, even when nothing particularly eventful or out of the ordinary is happening. You likely feel a good deal of anxiety and worry about things that haven't even happened yet and may never happen.

I wouldn't be surprised if you have significant trouble in your relationships, personal and/or professional. You're constantly on the lookout for something to go wrong. You might have difficulty with anger management, often perceiving yourself as a human punching bag and then feeling the need to retaliate. I would venture a guess that you experienced some significant trauma in childhood that hasn't healed yet—maybe it was neglect or abuse by your parents or other significant people involved in caring for you. You may at times feel as if your life is out of control, especially if you scored at the higher end of this range.

If you've never considered yourself to be a drama queen and you scored in this range, you might be thrown off guard and may even feel assaulted, if not insulted. If so, let me please try to comfort you and remind you that you're not a freak or defective. Not only can you overcome the over-reactivity that doesn't serve you well, but you owe it to yourself to get a new perspective. You deserve to have more peace and tranquility in your life. Of course, if you *are* truly in the middle of a crisis where you *are* in some real danger, you might have an elevated score. For instance, if you are going through a high-conflict divorce where your ex is threatening to take your kids from you by lying about your mental capacity, you're bound to be hyper-reactive because you're truly in a state of high stress. So you may have more of a situational-induced drama queen syndrome. But you can still benefit from the information that lies ahead since you may actually discover that you have a role in keeping crises alive. In other words, by taking more control over your emotions, you may become better equipped to handle whatever crisis you might be in now and in the future.

Score 76–100: Level Four

If you scored in this range, you're clearly in a state of over-reactivity a good chunk of the time. And my guess is that you also have great difficulty distinguishing events that are truly harmful from those that are harmless. You may have very few intimate friendships as people find you far too difficult to be around. More than likely you're well aware of this problem and desperately crave new tools to help you.

Please don't despair. You can absolutely make positive changes. But I do recommend that you also seek outside professional help as soon as possible, as the resources provided in this book won't be enough. Also, whatever you do, don't go into a shame hole. Instead, take immediate action and use all resources available to you for help. You can change your life if you claim responsibility for it. You will find Melissa's story in Chapter Three particularly helpful since it's a tale about one young woman's transformation from a Level Four drama queen to a "go-with-the-flow" gal. So be brave and make a serious vow to take charge of your healing!

Hope

Ideally, you've gathered by now that you shouldn't feel embarrassed or ashamed for the style in which you've learned to respond to the world. You haven't known a better way. But it's now time to give yourself the gift of tranquility. Also, as I shared with you in the Introduction, I'm no stranger to the drama queen syndrome. Thus, I have firsthand knowledge of how over-reactivity can affect one's life and it's usually not that pretty. However, some aspects of being a drama queen are delightful and these features don't require any changes. For example, there's certainly no harm in reacting with over-the-top excitement at a child's first step. It pleases the child and your body vibrates with joy. Who cares if this is an exaggeration! The key is to be in charge of these feelings and not have the feelings take charge of you.

So read through all the stories, do the exercises, and put your new learning into practice right away. You may be resistant to change, even fearful of it. But the good news is that even though you may feel as if you're going through an identity change—and you will be to some extent—you can always call upon your inner drama queen when needed. And when you don't need him or her, your alter ego self can rest quietly.

The Problem

I recommend that you start to play with your image of yourself. After all, whether you're aware of it or not, your personality is like a palette of different colors. But in order to paint a beautiful rainbow, there needs to be a skilled artist who knows how to blend the colors just right for the desired effect. So let's start training your inner artist to turn your drama queen into one of the many colors in a rainbow.

Chapter 2

How We Become Drama Queens

Drama Queens: Born or Made?

We are forever grappling with the age-old question of nature versus nurture. In this case, we're asking whether drama queens pop right out of the womb or whether they become overly sensitive and hyper-reactors because of their environment and the experiences they endure in childhood. Or, as is the case with most things in life, could the drama queen syndrome result from a combination of both nature and nurture?

While I wish I had a definitive answer for you on this one, I don't. However, I can say with confidence (due to more than 20 years of experience working with people who come to therapy for all sorts of issues) that I strongly believe that the drama queen syndrome results from a combination of temperament (which is dominantly inherited) *and* how the environment interplays and interacts with our personality styles. For some people who suffer from over-reactivity, it's because their genes made them ripe and ready for becoming a drama queen and their environment added fuel to the fire. For others, they developed their style because they endured so much drama and trauma that anyone in their situation would likely have become a drama queen. Of course, there are those select few who have gone through hell and high water and no matter what they've endured, they still walk through life peaceful and happy, as though they don't have a care in the world. (Or, perhaps they're really just in denial.)

Let me be a bit more specific. For instance, some kids come into the world far more extroverted than others, whereas some show up with a much more introverted style. Neither one is better than the other, just different. Also, some infants seem inherently anxious and tentative whereas others demonstrate a calm and easygoing demeanor, regardless of their environment. Some babies cry louder than others when they don't get the breast or the bottle quickly enough or when they don't like the way they're being burped or held. Other little ones don't seem to flinch no matter how you handle them; they're just content to be held. These differences exemplify the variability in temperament.

While basic temperament appears to be dominantly predetermined, it can definitely be altered, depending upon how a child grows up. Basically, who we ultimately end up becoming as adults is heavily affected and influenced by many factors, including parents, other significant caregivers, physical environment, media, and cultural influences. And while our childhood experiences make the biggest mark on how our identities develop, certain experiences in adulthood can also significantly affect our response style in the world and how we cope with life. So basically, we're always changing and adapting in response to our life experiences.

While we're ever-evolving beings, our childhoods (as opposed to our adulthood experiences) probably have the biggest influence on the development of our personalities and identities. Hence our early environment has a significant role in whether or not we develop the drama queen syndrome or at least the seeds for it to ripen later on. And these influences inevitably interact with hereditary or genetic influences, except for areas that are completely hard-wired like eye-color or genetic birth defects. Also, keep in mind that this statement isn't an absolute fact. I've worked with many people who've had relatively trauma-free childhoods, but who endured remarkably troubling experiences in adulthood, who then developed the drama queen syndrome.

While you may not really care too much about how a drama queen emerges and would rather jump right ahead to how to make changes (which by the way are definitely possible), please indulge me for a bit. I think you'll see that there's a good reason to understand the origins of the drama queen syndrome. While you may disagree, I firmly believe that by examining how the over-reactivity comes about, you can develop a more realistic expectation about what you can/cannot change about yourself and about how you interact with others in the world. So bear with me here and let me give you a couple of related examples to help you fully appreciate how complex this question of nature-versus-nurture is and how it applies to your understanding of the origins of becoming a drama queen.

Let's take physical characteristics as the first example. If a guy and gal are both well above average height and they choose to procreate, then most likely they're going to pass along their "tall" genes (again, we're talking heredity here, not hand-me-down pants!). If you're their kid, then the blueprint for your height would dictate that you will become a tall person. But let's say that gosh forbid your folks lost their jobs when you were an infant and became very limited in their ability to feed you properly. And just to be a bit more dramatic, let's say that you also get a severe intestinal bacterial infection which renders you ill with serious absorption and digestion problems. Your parents do the best they can, but you fail to receive the proper nourishment during your formative years and your growth gets stunted. Then, regardless of your DNA, you're likely to never reach your full height potential. (Thankfully, we don't have things like this happening too much in our country—but believe me, malnourishment continues to occur all over other parts of the world.) You can see how your genetics can easily be compromised by childhood traumas.

The Problem

There are lots of other examples where our genetics predispose us toward a certain characteristic but can then become altered by our environment. For instance, if a child is pre-programmed to be athletic but she eats too many burgers and French fries, never getting off her butt to exercise, then she's probably going to become overweight. Due to her own devices or lack of parental influence, she would likely prevent herself from ever reaching her full fitness potential. Or, if a child has a genetic blueprint for flawlessly smooth skin, but she trashes her *epidermis* (fancy word for skin) by sunbathing in the tropics without proper protection, thereby creating a deep-red lobster effect, she's bound to end up prematurely wrinkled and wishing she could turn back the clock.

On the flip side, sometimes compromised genetics can be reversed or minimized within a nurturing environment. For instance, take a child who's raised by alcoholics and who has three generations of family members with some form of addiction or mental disorder. This could seem like a formula for disaster. Yet many kids who come from a long line of addictions manage to create a healthy lifestyle for themselves and never develop a substance-abuse problem. Or maybe you've heard of or know someone who was diagnosed early on with autism. Many people have viewed this as a life sentence of institutionalization. Yet with recent advances in the understanding and treatment of developmental disorders, many autistic children have grown up to become fairly independent, functioning adults.

These are some pretty severe examples, but even so, you can see how blurred the distinctions can become around which has greater influence in how we turn out—nature or nurture. And the picture gets even blurrier when it comes to understanding behavior and personality styles. Since you picked up this book searching for tools specific to understanding the drama queen in you or in someone you love, I won't belabor the generalities of psychology too much. But hang in there with me just a bit more and read on for few more examples illustrating that change is very possible, but also that we need to be realistic and understand that nature does have some level of influence in our basic temperament and may limit *how* much and *what* we can change.

I'll use myself as an example of a drama queen made, not born. I came into this world according to my parents as extremely shy. My mom, who is sadly now deceased, used to tell me stories about how I would cling to her leg as a toddler anytime a new person came around. I didn't want others to hold me and would cry if anyone outside of my immediate circle of caregivers would approach me. But within my own circle of loved ones, I was very easygoing and adaptable. I wasn't outgoing, extroverted, or adventurous. But I was curious and exploratory. I was even described as very quiet (God knows, that's changed!).

As I grew up, however, I became extremely sensitive to my surrounding and reactive to everyone else's feelings. And without going into too much detail suffice it to say that my youth brought with it many traumas and events that frightened me and caused me to become even more externally anxious and over-reactive. Though there's no way of really knowing whether I would have developed these characteristics and resulting behaviors had I not gone through the turmoil I endured, I'm going to venture a guess that I developed the drama queen syndrome to a moderate level because of my environment. But I would also say that my having started out as a very sensitive and somewhat anxious child in temperament fostered a greater likelihood that I would move in that direction. Now, I'm much less shy, much more extroverted, and far less over-reactive to the ups and downs of daily life. And I attribute these changes primarily due to my own efforts and work toward self-growth. Melissa's story in the next chapter will illustrate this type of transformation in much greater detail and hopefully give you the confidence that no matter how bleak things may seem to you right now, you can make your life better.

I have also known people who were probably far more drama queenish right from the womb. I had a friend whose baby seemed to be in a constant state of fear when nothing had ever happened to him to warrant such anxiety. He just seemed born with this type of temperament. But with the loving nurturance of his two very wonderfully patient parents, he never developed the drama queen syndrome—lucky for him. As you know though, since you're reading this, we're not all so fortunate.

Nevertheless, my main point is to help you understand that it's very hard to know precisely the proportions of the drama queen syndrome that come from nature versus how much ends up the result from the way you were raised. Chances are if you're born with a certain type of temperament, you're not going to change your whole personality just by practicing the tools in this book. But, you definitely can move more in the direction of peace and tranquility.

So while you may not really care about how your drama queen syndrome evolved, in my experience, having recognition of influences that created an issue you're dealing with helps to heal these challenges and empowers you with new choices on how to react and act in the present. And, if you haven't already thought about it, there's a good chance that you'll be able to make some links that make sense to you about how you developed your issues. So with that in mind, below is a list and a description of the various environmental influences that may have contributed to your drama queen syndrome.

Please note that I'm not directing you toward examining your life experiences to promote blaming of others for who you are today. Everything in this book is aimed at building your sense of empowerment and toward directing you to take full responsibility for your life in the present so that you can ultimately create a response style that is flexible in the situations you become faced with. No longer do you have to be a prisoner to reactions that control you. Very rarely in life are we ever true victims, so it's important to start looking at your life from today forward as a series of choices and options. Don't worry if you don't believe me now or if it doesn't make sense. I trust that this will all come into much clearer focus and make much more sense to you as you continue reading and start doing the recommended exercises.

How We Become Drama Queens

Origins of the Drama Queen Syndrome

Now that you understand that nature, particularly with regards to our temperament, may have a contributing influence in developing the drama queen syndrome, we can now move on to identifying the more obvious environmental contributors.

Keep in mind that most people have had a multitude of traumas, drama, or losses contributing to their tendencies to overreact, to becoming too sensitive, and/or to having trouble chilling out and going with the flow. Then again, there are some people who only suffered a few traumas that may not even be considered such a big deal and still they became drama queens. But because these folks didn't have any support or healing for things they endured, whatever they did go through had a huge impact. And far be it from me to judge what things should or shouldn't be a big deal to someone. We all have different levels of resiliency depending on other factors in our lives. For instance, one child may have been mildly abused, and in turn, he develops a severe level of the drama queen syndrome because he didn't have any other loving caregivers to buffer the blows. In contrast, another child may have been severely abused, but she weathers childhood with great strength and only a few repercussions because she was fortunate enough to have several influential loving and stable caregivers. So don't be hard on yourself, just try to recognize what's fitting for you.

If you're the significant other who is reading this, please use this list to deepen your understanding of your loved one. It's my experience that the more we understand the origins of how something comes about, the more we build compassion and empathy because we then stop personalizing the annoying behavior and we can actually become part of the solution. And, if you happen to be the parent of a budding or full-fledged drama queen, try not to be too hard on yourself if you recognize that you may have made some serious parenting errors. *No one* is a perfect parent and we all make mistakes. Just acknowledge your errors and make amends whenever possible.

The Problem

Please also keep in mind that this list is hardly exhaustive. Since each of us has a unique history, it would be impossible to include every nuance of someone's life. So if I haven't included something you think is connected to your syndrome, please don't feel slighted. You're experience is perfectly valid, even if I've inadvertently omitted it. Plus, these explanations are broad categories, with a few examples, not specifically detailed accounts. You might think a category relates to you, but then you read the examples and believe it no longer applies—that may not mean it is not relevant. I just may have missed the specific relevance to your life so try to find the overlap. And, at the end of this chapter there's an exercise to help you put together the pieces of your own life's puzzle. Hopefully, some of the items and examples included will help you connect the dots in your own life.

Just one more thing to keep in mind. Though it may appear that I've listed these in some objective or scientifically determined order of importance, I haven't. Of course, many people commonly believe that certain experiences would definitely have bigger wounding power than others. For instance, most people would think that a pre-pubescent child molested by her own father would experience more psychological and emotional distress than an adolescent boy who got slugged a few times by a bully in the schoolyard. But this is not always the case. Whether something has the potential to generate the drama queen syndrome depends on so many other factors in combination. Using the above example, the child who was molested by her dad may actually fare much better than the bullied teenager if her mom hauled up and left the father and got her daughter into whatever therapy was needed. Or, the young girl still might have been better off had the teenage boy's dad told his son that the bully should have left him for dead because he was a "good for nothing" son.

Be open to all possibilities of discovery and don't feel bad if you think what happened to you "shouldn't" be such a big deal. If it was, then it was. Remember the motto: no shame, no blame. Just accept what is. The good news in the end is that once you make meaningful discoveries about the historical links to your drama queen syndrome, you can then leave these in the past where they belong and no longer continue to carry your baggage into your present adult life.

Now, as promised, onward to the list.

1. abuse from caregivers
2. abuse from outside influences
3. sibling rivalry
4. garden-variety family dysfunction
5. role-modeling
6. relationship drama (friendship versus intimate)
7. trauma and loss

Abuse from Caregivers

Abuse can come in many different varieties, including physical, sexual, and mental/emotional. I also include neglect and abandonment in this category. Though not necessarily the same as an abusive action toward a child, the absence of care while a child is entirely dependent on others for his/her needs can ultimately be as abusive as being beaten by an out-of-control, raging caregiver on a daily basis, especially if the rageful parent offers moments of kindness.

When any of these horrible atrocities happen to a child by his/her caregivers, the results can be devastating. Commonly, children who are abused by their caregivers end up with deep trust issues, low self-esteem and, not surprisingly, a vigilance toward safety in fear of danger. After all, children don't have the same choices that adults have and are at times completely powerless in the world. Hence, they must rely on others to keep them from harm's way. So if the very people who are supposed to protect a child are the same ones who are hurting him or potentially putting him in danger, then the child can't do anything about it, except to rely on innate survival skills. In other words, the child can't outright divorce himself from his family, so he has to create whatever coping mechanisms are necessary to stay alive in the situation he's in. For many people this translates into becoming hyper-vigilant to safety—a common feature of the drama queen syndrome.

Alison, a charming and very funny twenty-eight-year-old woman, endured repeated physical abuse by her mother. Usually the blows would come when the mother would perceive Alison as being disrespectful. The mother would first start raising her voice, aiming to frighten Alison. Alison would become very quiet—a reaction which her mother would perceive as being even more disrespectful. This would frustrate the heck out of the mother and then she'd start slapping Alison wherever her hands would fall, sometimes to the point of leaving bruises and welts. This form of discipline went on throughout Alison's early teens. Then at around age fifteen, Alison stood up to her mother (actually slapping her back) and threatened to report her to child protective services.

"Where the heck was her dad in all of this?" you might be wondering. Sadly, even though he lived in the same home, Alison's father was too much of a wimp to intervene on his daughter's behalf. Rather than protect Alison from her mother's abuse, he actually blamed Alison, telling her that she needed to behave better.

As an adult, though Alison no longer had to endure her mother's abuse or her father's blame, she continued to have a very strong reaction to anyone who raised a voice above a soft whisper. Okay, maybe the drama queen in me is embellishing a little—Alison could tolerate normal decibels, but anything approaching what others might consider mild animation caused her great anxiety. And thus, she had developed a zero tolerance policy for conflict, avoiding anything that even remotely smelled of the potential for discord, at all costs. As you can well imagine, not being able to handle anything to do with a conflict seriously affected Alison's relationships with others, especially since almost every close relationship hits a bump in the road now and again. And, no doubt, she was frequently accused of being a drama queen.

Tom, a forty-year-old father of three kids and very successful businessman, endured continual emotional abuse from his stepfather. His own dad had died when he was only four years old (his sister was six) and because his mother was financially unstable and didn't think she could make it on her own with two young kids to raise and no man to help her, she married the first guy who came her way who promised to give her the "life she deserved." Oh, what a mistake. Though he spread a pretty set of peacock feathers during their courting phase, he showed his true colors of black and blacker once she said "I do." From that moment forward it was all downhill.

This stepfather berated everyone in the house, reducing them to tears on a daily basis. Although Tom was but a little boy, he wanted to protect his mother and would often shift the focus onto himself when his stepfather would go after his mother. He would either start acting out so that the attention would turn to him or he would try to become the family clown and diffuse the situation by making everyone laugh. Poor Tom, what a burden to have to bear. Sometimes his clowning around would do the trick. Step-daddy-dearest would actually lighten up and allow himself to be entertained. But inevitably he would cycle back to his miserable, jerky behavior.

During times while the step-dad wasn't around, Tom would work overtime trying to get his mother's attention. Sadly, she was far too preoccupied to notice. All she could think about was what a mistake she'd made by marrying this a-hole, and she spent hours each day contemplating how she was going to fix the mess she'd gotten herself and her kids into. Of course, she never found an answer and she stayed with this creep, leaving her kids subjected to this emotional and psychological assault throughout their entire youth.

Tom's only means of getting any nurturance from his mom was to exaggerate everything—both the good and the bad. He became the master embellisher. And naturally he took this coping style with him when he flew the coop at nineteen. Luckily for Tom, he never lost his creative spirit and he became very successful in his career path without even going to college. But while he certainly elicited many laughs from his peers and from partygoers, he had a very hard time having successful long-term intimate relationships since he had never had a good role model for healthy love.

Tom had hoped that his marriage to Nora would yield a better outcome. He truly loved her and wanted to grow old with her. But, because of what he endured in childhood (something he never adequately dealt with), Tom wasn't able to keep his marriage together because he had no idea how to handle inevitable discord. Whenever he experienced the first sign of conflict or something he believed would become a problem, he would either resort to his clownlike behavior (not able to be serious when the situation called for it), or he would get far more animated than the situation warranted, and sometimes even rageful. His wife couldn't handle the huge ups and downs. And even though she begged for him to get help, he wouldn't. After seven years, she filed for a divorce.

Thankfully, Tom got himself into therapy, though too late to save his marriage. And once he was able to connect the dots between his childhood abuse and his resulting drama queen syndrome, he was able to choose new and more adaptive styles to deal with the inevitable progressions and setbacks in his adult life. He wasn't being emotionally abused anymore, but before he got the help he needed, he reacted to almost everyone and everything as though he were still a little boy trapped in a horror movie. He finally came to recognize that life was pretty good and didn't require so much micromanaging and hyper-reactivity.

How We Become Drama Queens

Abuse from Outside Influences

Although abuse by one's own caregivers or family members usually results in the most long-term harm and problems in adulthood, that's certainly not always the case. In fact, sometimes the effects may even be more severe when someone experiences abuse from people outside one's family, resulting in less than ideal coping mechanisms and overall well-being.

For instance, Lisa had been repeatedly sexually abused (fondling, kissing, inappropriate touching) by a soccer coach trusted in the community. She had told her parents what was happening to her, but they didn't believe her. To Lisa's discredit, she had a history of embellishing the truth, and, at times, telling outright lies. Her parents weren't neglectful or abusive (though they were fairly naïve to have completely dismissed her claims and not even attempt to investigate such an accusation); they just chalked up her disclosures as just another one of her manipulative schemes to get attention. Of course as is common of child molesters, Lisa's coach outwardly displayed a charming and highly likeable demeanor. And, no one else was complaining about him. So no one would have even been suspicious of him. But privately, he was abusing Lisa, scaring her into believing that if she ever told anyone, he'd harm someone in her family. She was only seven and this went on for two years.

As it turned out, Lisa eventually talked her parents into letting her quit the soccer team. But she never got them to believe her "story." To deal with her pain, she entered into a performing arts track all the way through her schooling. And this helped soothe her to some extent. But because she never got proper attention for her trauma, she overreacted to just about everything. When she married and had children of her own, she became extremely overprotective and unable to relax concerning anything involving the care of her kids. For instance, she spent the first five years of her firstborn daughter's life never leaving her in anyone's care other than with a close family member. And, even those times were very rare, since she wouldn't trust anyone to watch them. Inadvertently, Lisa created a negative spiral because, while her intentions were to protect her daughter, she rarely ever allowed herself to get a break from her parenting role. Hence, she was constantly stressed out.

Lisa's over-reactivity didn't stop there. Rather, she pretty much went into a tizzy anytime she had to deal with a change in schedule or an unexpected event. Fortunately, however, once she was able to understand the impact of her childhood abuse on her present functioning, she was able to start giving her kids and herself more breathing room.

Abuse from outside sources comes in many varieties from physical to emotional to sexual, and can be inflicted by any number of people such as: relatives, babysitters, teachers, schoolyard bullies, peers, or even passing strangers, as in the case of being mugged while walking to school or being gang-raped in a dark alley. Sometimes it can be very subtle, but no less devastating, as in the case of a child who is repeatedly teased and humiliated by a group of kids at school who think they're better than everyone else but who are actually more like losers than winners. While not everyone has a story like Lisa's, if you were abused by someone outside of your immediate caregiver circle, please don't minimize the impact if it truly affected you in any way.

Sibling Rivalry

Who would think that squabbles with your little brother, big sister, or any other sibling combination could have any relevance to the drama queen syndrome? Well actually it's not a far stretch of the imagination at all if you consider how much time and energy you spend interacting with your sibs throughout childhood. Plus, we often seek as much approval and admiration from our siblings as we do our adult caregivers. The scenarios as to how sibling rivalry might contribute to becoming a drama queen are endless. But here's a few to consider and maybe one or more of these will help you solve your own puzzle.

1. Your sibling was the favorite child of one or both of your parents and you felt the need to do cartwheels around the house (don't take this metaphor too literally), or else you feared you'd be completely dismissed.

2. Your sibling was truly better at a number of things valued by society—doing well at school, achieving in athletics, having lots of friends—and you didn't get enough attention because you didn't demonstrate any qualities your parents or society found to be admirable.

3. Your sibling had physical characteristics which commanded a lot of positive attention from others and you weren't noticed for your assets.

4. Your sibling put you down or made you the scapegoat where you were seen as being at fault for any conflicts, which arose even when you were actually innocent.

These are but a few of the many scenarios that might leave a child feeling as though he or she isn't very important. And because we all need our fair share of attention and admiration, if we're not getting enough of it from the people closest to us, we become ripe candidates for developing the drama queen syndrome.

If you grew up with siblings, older or younger, think back for a moment or two as to whether you may be carrying around any sore spots concerning your sibling relationships.

Garden-Variety Family Dysfunction

I simply had to throw this category in here to make the point that truly anything could have the potential to create a drama queen. Since drama queens are noted for their over-reactivity it's easy to see how abuse and neglect would have a direct cause-and-effect relationship to the drama queen syndrome. That doesn't mean I'm suggesting that you should feel sorry for yourself or remain a victim to your previous childhood experiences. What I am saying, however, is that in your quest to understand the specific origins of your own emotional suffering, hypersensitivity, and over-reactive response style you should be open-minded about looking at all possibilities. Again, this is not a prescription to do the "woe is me" thing, but rather, a recommendation that you use this information as something to help give a context to your discomfort.

So yes, even if your caregivers weren't abusive or neglectful, you may still have developed an over-reactive style because of some other (less-toxic) family dynamic. In other words, even if your caregivers were fantastic parents in your mind and their intentions were always good, all families have some dysfunction. So if your caregivers were too lenient, too strict, too impulsive, too withholding of affection, too critical, or too whatever, it's important to figure out how their style of parenting may have set you up to become a drama queen. But remember, don't do that blame thing where you point the finger and say something like, "Well there you have it—my parents did (fill in the blank) so that's why I'm screwed up." No, no, no. Instead, say something more like, "Well look at that, I experienced x, y, and z and I didn't get the tools I needed to know how to distinguish true danger from something I can actually cope with. Now I know what holes I need to fill and I can learn new ways to respond to the world."

Lorena's mom was a control freak and needed everything to be put in its place or she would have a hissy fit. Lorena's sister didn't seem affected by this at all, but Lorena felt she needed to be extra cautious around her mother. She developed a fairly profound drama queen syndrome such that she could pretty much identify with everything on the self-assessment tool from Chapter One, bringing her to Level Three on the drama-queen-syndrome scale. It's not that Lorena's mom was mean or anything, actually she was kind and generous. But she simply had to have everything in its place and things done properly. Though Lorena's mother thought she was instilling good manners and raising well-behaved kids (and she was), because Lorena was very sensitive and in need of her mom's approval, she ended up feeling like she could never do anything right. As an adult, Lorena felt the need to pick on herself about all sorts of things, from the way she dressed to the way she held a cup. As a result she could never feel "right" with herself. And anytime something went wrong or off-center a bit she would go into her "Oh my God, I'm so sorry" mode, blaming herself for anything and everything and, then, wanting to make everything better.

Poor Lorena couldn't just simply chill out and let things be. Rather, she spent most of her energy making sure everyone else's needs were met and forgetting about her own, thereby running on empty much of the time. Of course when "real" issues would arise, she's be so maxed out that all she could do was just become exasperated and overdramatic. No worries, though. She eventually learned how to go with the flow and let people take care of themselves. And she also came to realize that her mother's anxiety and need to keep everything in her world a certain way had nothing to do with Lorena's value as a person.

Role-Modeling

Children, and even young adults, learn about the world and themselves through observing others around them. They often parrot or copy others' influential behavior and they develop their attitudes and beliefs based on these role models. Even their identities get shaped through observing others around them. In the previous example, Lorena's mom conveyed her perfectionism and need to have everything in a certain order usually using a very sweet tone, without any hysteria. She was very controlled. And she didn't have the reactive style associated with drama queens. There are many others caregivers like Lorena's mom who are driven by anxiety. But, unlike Lorena's mom, who would keep her reactions in check, others react with a drama queen's style. As the saying goes in these situations, "The apple doesn't fall far from the tree." While it certainly isn't always the case that a child will mimic a parent or other influential caregiver's behavior, many kids will learn their coping skills from what they observe in others.

If you had a parent who overreacted to things fairly regularly, it shouldn't surprise you to discover that you may have developed the same coping style simply because of the process of imitation. And it may not even occur to you that all situations don't require big reactions. But now, you can learn that what monkey sees, monkey doesn't have to do!

Parents aren't the only source of our learned coping styles. Many people rely heavily on media influences. So if you were a kid who was planted in front of the TV as a form of babysitting, it's possible you learned some of your drama queen tendencies and behaviors from characters from your favorite shows. Many other institutions (cultural, social, religion) may have also been contributors to your reactionary style.

Relationships

Let's face it. Most of us have had a relationship or two in our lives that didn't go so well. But some people have had multiple intimate bonds that have gone seriously south, filled with anguish and heartache. Naturally, if you experienced rejection, humiliation, or threats of abandonment during your childhood, it's likely that you may have become overly sensitive and constantly fearful of bad things happening to you. Therefore, it would not be surprising if your relationships would inevitably become filled with a lot of drama.

Mind you, some of these relationships may have actually been bad news, regardless of your contributions. After all, it's very likely that we will re-create relationships in adulthood that mimic the feelings we experienced in our childhood relationships. If we haven't healed old wounds, we're liable to become magnets for more pain and suffering in adulthood.

But sometimes, we will attract *positive* people in our lives, despite left-over negative energy. And if we suffer from the drama queen syndrome, we're highly likely to unknowingly sabotage these bonds as well.

Note: I'm not in any way suggesting that the drama is all your doing. It takes two to tango. So don't be too hard on yourself. But do try to reflect back honestly and thoughtfully on your relationships (intimate ones and friendships) that have resulted in termination, and acknowledge the ones where you may have contributed a disproportionate amount of drama.

Traumas and Loss

If things happen to us unexpectedly and/or when we're not developmentally able to cope with the experience, we can become seriously scarred and very frightened of the world. I've worked with many lovable drama queens who've suffered significant trauma in their lives and, sadly, they've lacked the support necessary to process their pain and move through it. Even if we are developmentally capable of handling certain events, sometimes the experience is so devastating, there's no way not to become overly sensitive and reactive.

Traumas can be physical, as in breaking a leg or becoming seriously ill, or emotional, as in going through the death of a loved one or of having the man or woman of your dreams dump you for someone else. Some traumas are long-lasting, as in the case of dying of lung cancer. Others are short-lived, as in the case of getting hit by an out-of-control vehicle traveling 60 mph. But short-lived traumas often have long-term consequences. Sometimes the fallout from a trauma can be even more devastating than the trauma itself, as in the case of a woman who gets through a rape without physical damage and doesn't contract an STD or get mutilated or physically harmed in any way. But for this woman, the repercussions to her sexual life may far outweigh the actual rape if she's never able to achieve orgasm, even with a loving partner, because she believes she is unworthy of sexual pleasure and she perceives herself as "damaged goods."

The Problem

Often, if someone gets dealt a really bad hand and has to endure a series of traumas or losses, he or she becomes a highly likely candidate for becoming a member of the drama queen club. Sandy, for instance, a very attractive and dynamic young woman, suffered multiple losses between the ages of five and ten, including the death of her mother. Her father wasn't able to soothe or comfort her as he himself had to deal with his own grief. She felt so lost and alone and had no way of knowing how to get through her pain. Later in life when even the slightest thing would go wrong, Sandy would act as if her house were on fire. And because she felt so threatened that she would lose people she loved, she was constantly taking the emotional temperature of her relationships with her friends. She couldn't accept anything at face value without reading into it some deeper—usually bad—meaning. For instance, if a friend cancelled dinner plans because of being too tired, Sandy would immediately assume that she'd done something wrong to piss off her friend and she would go on a mission to find out the truth. Of course, over time this annoyed the heck out of her friends. She would inevitably become such a pest and a pain in the butt because she couldn't just let things be. People actually really liked her; they just couldn't tolerate her excessive need for reassurance.

Personal List

I've simplified most the examples highlighted above in order to get you thinking about the kinds of things that may have contributed to your becoming a drama queen (or the one you love). In reality, people's lives are far more complex and rarely do any of our issues trace back to a single event or experience. In fact, all of our experiences interact with each other. Plus, our perceptions and memories of the events we experience continually get reshaped and they change over time. Some things will seem like a bigger deal than they actually were at the time of occurrence, and other things will seem less intense than they actually were as time has passed. So while I don't want you to dwell too much on belaboring the question of how you became a drama queen, do give some thought to what kinds of things you've experienced that may have created the anxiety or emotional turmoil that gets expressed in your behavior.

If you've already had some psychotherapy or you're currently seeking help, then you've probably done at least a little bit of this archeological dig into your past. But if not, and this is your first time even considering that the categories I mentioned above may actually have a connection to your drama queen syndrome, then please take out pen and paper, or get on the computer, if you prefer, and do a little journaling about the significant events or experiences that may have left you with some emotional wounds. Even if you can't recall anything of importance, then at the very least, look inward—close your eyes and ask yourself: "Why is it that I can't seem to just chill out and relax?" And try answering this question with responses such as:

- I fear rejection.
- I'm afraid of danger.
- I feel out of control.
- I believe that no one will notice me if I'm not louder and more dramatic than everyone else.

Okay, now give it a go and see what you come up with. Then if you're up to it, make a list of your biggest traumas, your biggest fears, and your most significant losses. Once you've identified all of these, spend a few moments empathizing with whatever you've gone through but without blaming others. It's now time to accept that it's your job to let go of the old pain and allow your life in the present to determine how you react from here forward.

Unless you're currently in an abusive or self-destructive situation or truly in danger, then you no longer have to react to the world as though you're still a child without choices and options. And when things you fear actually happen, you will have far more energy to deal with them than if you continue using up your resources for life's ongoing ups and downs. Also, the purpose of checking in with yourself about the origins of your over-reactivity is simple: when you're more in touch with your inner world of feelings and thoughts, you become more empowered to change any behavior that doesn't serve you well. So congratulations on taking that first step!

Chapter 3

Melissa's Story: Finding the Diamond in the Rough

To better understand how to transform a *drama* queen into a much more *serene* queen (or king, if you so prefer), let's meet Melissa. Her story depicts, in detail, the full process of becoming an over-reactor, living as one, and then finally seeing the light—that is that life can be much more enjoyable and relaxing without all the drama. Hers is a story of truly turning chicken shit into chicken salad; or if you'd rather have the G-rated description—of turning lemons into lemonade. Hopefully her tale will help take away any shame or embarrassment you may be carrying for being a drama queen and highlight how you can become fully in charge of how you respond to life's curve balls.

As you read on, keep in mind that Melissa's story is but one example of a drama queen. Her experience won't be reflective of everyone's, so please don't turn this into a competition. You may believe your situation is much worse than Melissa's and be tempted to dismiss any similarity. Or, you may think your experience doesn't even come close to her suffering and then conclude that you're just acting like a child or making a mountain out of a molehill. Neither of these interpretations will do you any good. So please try to refrain from qualitative comparisons. Don't minimize the importance of your suffering should you believe that Melissa's life has been far more out-of-control than your life. And vice versa. If you believe you're in an even worse predicament than Melissa, don't convince yourself that there's nothing for you to relate to.

Again, there isn't one type of drama queen or one recipe for creating one. They come in all varieties. There's simply not enough space to be able to give an example of each. Even if there were, I'd still fall short because there's so many of you I've never had the pleasure of meeting! But I do hope that Melissa's story reflects enough commonalities that you will feel encouraged to truly embark on a life filled with much more tranquility, and that you will learn to accept that you can *choose* when and how to make it more exciting, if you so desire.

I take extra care in stating these precautions because drama queens notoriously believe that no one could possibly understand their particular situation. If this describes you, you're likely to only focus on how this story doesn't apply to you. For example, if you're married and you find that Melissa is not even in a relationship, you might dismiss the message because you don't share this in common. But marital status is irrelevant to understanding and transforming the drama queen syndrome, as are many other characteristics used to define people—they simply don't have any weight. So please refrain from ruling out commonalities because the surrounding variables such as age, parental status, sexual preference, family background, or employment status are quite different.

Chances are you're in a lot of emotional pain right now and you may feel very alone in your suffering (whether you're the identified drama queen or the person who cares about one). If you're the drama queen, maybe you've just lost a relationship because your intimate partner could no longer handle your exaggerated highs and lows. Or maybe you were just fired from a job because you were accused of creating too much drama. Or maybe you haven't lost anything and you're just beginning to open up to the idea that you may be a part of the problems in your life—that you're not a complete victim—and now you're seeking a solution before things get out of hand. Whatever drove you to this book doesn't matter. I'm just glad it did. So whether you'd like to admit it or not, you do share similarities with other drama queens—maybe not necessarily in terms of the content (in how your drama queen syndrome is expressed) but certainly with regards to how it affects the quality of your life and your relationships.

If you're the significant other of a drama queen, you're probably at your wit's end by now and may even be on the verge of dumping the relationship altogether. You may be the parent of a drama queen and wish to cut all ties, though you won't because you don't want to abandon your child. Or maybe you're the adult child of a drama queen parent, and you feel more like the parent in the relationship. Whatever your particulars might be, I caution you to please not be hasty. You, too, may actually discover that the situation isn't nearly as bleak as you imagine. Now please read on with a focus on Melissa's *process* of transformation rather than on the details of her life.

Melissa's Story

Melissa, a charming, endearing, and very bright thirty-one-year-old teacher most definitely had a rough go in life. Her parents divorced when she was ten and she was left in the primary care of her mother. Though things certainly weren't rosy before then, they got a great deal worse once her dad was out of the picture.

During her first decade of life, Melissa's parents were at war. They fought constantly, hurling verbal assaults back and forth as though they were playing an aim-to-kill tennis match. Melissa feared they'd either end up dead or divorced. Fortunately they didn't kill one another, but their relationship dissolved in an uproar, with Melissa's dad storming out. And while he continued to have contact with Melissa through phone calls and letters, he rarely ever resurfaced for face-to-face visits throughout the rest of Melissa's youth. He simply couldn't endure the custody battle Melissa's mom threatened. Basically, he believed he had no choice but to throw in the towel.

Though Melissa's dad was clearly no saint, he was by far the more stable of her two parents (at least by outside appearance). Once he bailed, which added a dimension of severe abandonment to Melissa's list of traumas, Melissa had no buffer of sanity. She did, however, manage to reconnect and repair bonds with him in adulthood—more on this later.

Melissa's mother, Jan, was a tyrant. Rather than opting to be a parent, she should have become a military drill sergeant. Though come to think of it, she might have even been considered too tough for the armed forces. She knew nothing about empathy, compassion, or soothing. If Melissa came to her with a problem, she'd either laugh at her or tell her to figure it out herself. Jan blamed Melissa for Jackson's (the father) departure and she treated Melissa like a slave.

Jan's mistreatment of Melissa didn't stop at hostility and putdowns. She also added insult to injury by making Melissa do endless chores and meaningless tasks. She wasn't allowed to have friends over and, if she was even five minutes late when called down to dinner, she'd be punished with a two-hour-early bedtime. Melissa had no idea how to cope or what to do. Sounds a bit like *Cinderella*, doesn't it? But it's actually worse since Jan was her birth mother and we'd like to believe that a biological caregiver would at least want to have some bond with a child she chose to raise.

In spite of Jan's horrific treatment toward her, Melissa endlessly sought her mother's approval, while simultaneously living in constant fear of her mother's wrath. Not surprisingly, despite Melissa's attempts to dance to a tune her mother would admire, Jan wouldn't budge from her harsh stance. She was far too self-centered to recognize the emotional pain she caused for anyone around her, particularly her own daughter. I certainly wouldn't be surprised to discover that Jan had severe narcissistic personality disorder, an extreme version of self-centeredness and inability to empathize with others, though I must refrain from diagnosing her since I never actually met her in person. But I trust Melissa's description as being accurate, despite her drama queen syndrome.

To make matters worse, the only time Jan would even remotely demonstrate a bit of kindness toward Melissa was when they were out in public. Then Jan would create a façade of warmth so that she would not be seen for the witch she truly was. Essentially, Jan would temporarily act as though Melissa's needs and feelings mattered to her, until they were once again out of the public's view.

Thankfully, Melissa's loving and nurturing aunt from her father's side of the family periodically took her in during summer breaks while Jan vacationed out of town. At least Melissa got a little bit of tender loving care now and again—but certainly not enough to erase the ongoing damage being done to her self-esteem during the long consecutive months she would have to spend with her mother.

Sadly, Melissa grew to become leery of people. And she seriously doubted whether she could actually trust anyone to ever care for her. Not surprisingly, she learned early on to believe that caregivers don't actually have their children's best interest at heart. And because of this framework, she generalized this belief to people at large. Hence, once she began to establish relationships with others, she had difficulty trusting people she got close to. Also, because of her mother's constant nit-picking, Melissa forever feared that she was doing something wrong and was constantly on red alert for when she would be reprimanded, not just by her mother but also from teachers, peers, and other important people in her life. I'm surprised she didn't retreat from the human race altogether.

Melissa demonstrated tremendous resiliency and managed to keep on going without becoming suicidal. But not without tremendous struggle and hardship. Though she managed to pass all of her classes, she had a hard time concentrating on her schoolwork. She was desperate for some attention in whatever form she could get it. Are you guessing where this is going? Thought so. Yup—she started stirring up trouble among her peers—not because she wanted negative attention. Rather, she simply didn't know of any other kind.

In high school, Melissa became a big tease with the boys and she frequently flirted with other girls' boyfriends. While many peers referred to her as a "bitch" or a "prick-tease," she actually wasn't trying to be malicious. Of course, try to convince a girl whose crush accepted solicitous invitations from her so-called friend that there were no bad intentions. A tough feat.

Because Melissa didn't develop positive relationship skills, she really didn't know how to be a good friend to someone. As a result, she routinely sabotaged any potential true friendships she might have had. Because she had no idea how to transform her negative experiences from her home life into constructive life lessons, she continued to command the negative attention she had gotten used to from mommy dearest. Hence, she developed a reputation of being a troublemaker and she was constantly getting into fights with her girlfriends. After a while, she was ostracized by most of her peers and ended up feeling even lonelier and in more despair than if she'd never even sought out any friendships.

While she eventually could see how her upbringing significantly affected her life's choices, at that point, as a teenager, she had no idea that she was creating her own drama and that she actually had the power right at her own fingertips to get her needs met in more appropriate and effective ways. In fact, her life continued to become filled with so much chaos and upheaval, it would make the popular soap opera stars in *All My Children* or the guests on the *Jerry Springer Show* seem boring and mundane. Now *that's* drama.

Pretty much every day became another crisis, adding to the stress of the previous day's turmoil. And Melissa began feeling more and more like a victim, seeking pity from others around her. But it was hard for people to reach out to her because she'd stab them in the back. Plus, she overreacted to just about everything.

Were she not as intelligent as she is, she would probably have failed out of school. But fortunately she did get decent grades and managed to get into college where she earned a Bachelor of Arts degree and eventually went on to became an elementary-school teacher. But because of her drama queen syndrome, she encountered many problems at her workplace and was close to getting fired from several teaching positions.

Melissa had had a few intimate relationships but most ended in disaster. No matter how a guy treated her, she never felt loved or in receipt of enough attention. Also, she created problems when there weren't any, often then becoming very ashamed of her hysteria. But no one would believe her sincerity since her behavior never changed. As a result, she would plead and beg for forgiveness from her partner only to turn around in five minutes and have another exaggerated response to something trivial.

If someone were to chronicle a day-in-the-life of Melissa (from her voice) an entry might look something like this:

Got up, washed face, saw a pimple emerging. Panicked and immediately called dermatologist for emergency appointment. Can't show up to party tonight with a blemish! Oh my, what will I wear? I have nothing! (Of course, she would actually have about ten new outfits, still accessorized by the price tags.) *And the shoes—OMG—how will I find new shoes on such short notice? Okay, calm down. Plan—get a grip. No I can't calm down—too much to do!* (Phone rings) *Pete—thank God it's you. I thought it was going to be Fran who's now pissed off at me because I forgot to show up at her house last night. Give me a break, if only she knew how busy I am. What's up? No, no, no—I can't possibly be there by six tonight, I need four hours just to get ready. Do you want me to have a heart attack?*

Got to go to the bank—check bounced last week. OMG—credit will be tarnished for the rest of my life. Won't anyone cut me some slack? It's not my fault I forgot to deposit my paycheck. Jeez—I had a million other things to do. Ran into traffic, now late for hair appointment. Tonight will be ruined.

The Problem

Arrive at Pete's—(we'd settled on 7 p.m.) and go to the party. Talk to a few people—tell a couple of funny stories and get a laugh from a few strangers. Why don't my friends think I'm funny? They must not have a sense of humor.

The frenetic energy goes on and on!

If you were able to track Melissa all day long, you'd probably become exhausted—even if you happened to be a very well polished drama queen yourself. You'd see Melissa running around like a chicken without a head. And no matter what was going on around her, she'd react to it like she'd just been stung by a bee—no, actually make that twenty bee stings all at once.

One day, all hell broke loose. Melissa's mother had a car accident and was in the hospital and Melissa had no idea what to do. She wanted to see her mother, but she was also so angry at her and blamed her for all the problems in her life. Once Melissa had left home to attend college, she'd barely spoken to her mother. Though she had always secretly longed for some kind of relationship with her mom, she had convinced herself that she didn't need her because she couldn't tolerate the insults and criticisms she had to endure each time they had contact.

The news that her mom was in critical condition lying in a hospital bed sent Melissa over the edge. She couldn't handle the emotional turmoil of a real crisis, possibly concerning life or death. Thankfully, Melissa recognized that it was time for her to get some help. Her life was out of control. By the way, she did go visit her mom—even hooked up to all kinds of monitors, Jan still couldn't help but be hostile and difficult.

Melissa's Transformation

The day Melissa finally landed herself in therapy, her world started to open up to new possibilities. About a year prior to coming to my office, she'd had an inkling that she might need to learn how to manage stress and how not to take things so personally. On the advice of one of the few friends she managed to keep in her life, she attempted to take a few yoga classes and she bought a couple of books on stress management. She even sought the counsel of several psychotherapists. But none of these efforts paid off because they weren't addressing the core problems. As a result, she felt even more frustrated with the world and her life. And, in turn, she became even more hopeless and entrenched in her drama queen syndrome. Thankfully, she didn't give up completely, and she dialed yet one more phone number in a desperate attempt to get her life together.

Believe me, I'm certainly not taking full credit for her profound improvements. Yes, Melissa and I certainly made a good team for tackling her drama queen syndrome. But it was Melissa who ultimately did all the work. Essentially, it was the fact that Melissa found it in her to admit that something was wrong with her life and how she was living it *and* that is was up to *her* to do something about changing and learning to *choose* her actions rather than simply being a punching bag swinging back and forth to the rhythmic jabs of life's left hooks. I just helped her through the process and guided her on a journey of healing, by helping her let go of the past, building her ability to self-care, and helping her to just chill out. I'm so glad I was able to accurately assess her issues and provide her with the care she needed.

So here's how her transformation came about. At first, the road to her discoveries and eventual changes came with tremendous stress and resistance. As is often the case with drama queens, Melissa's therapy initially resembled her life—filled with drama, upsets, turmoil, and angst. Sometimes it seemed as though she hated me, sometimes she seemed to think I was as cool as the invention of cell phones. She would either get enraged or very hurt whenever I tried to point out that she was actually the one who needed to change. I had to convince her that, even if the rest of the world stayed exactly the same, she'd be okay as long as she took charge of her reactions to life's events.

This was like a message from hell for Melissa. "It's the rest of the world that needs to change," she would say. "I'm just a victim to so many hardships," "I can't possibly be responsible for being late everywhere, there's just too much traffic," "How can I possibly be creating my own stress," would be common thoughts she would say or ponder. Essentially, Melissa couldn't see her own role in her unhappiness and agitation. She wanted to blame everyone and everything outside of herself for why she was in a constant state of stress and reactivity. For at least several months, she couldn't even fathom that she might actually be the writer, producer, and actor of her very own soap opera of a life. And then it took some more time for her to actually embrace the notion that she had the power to re-write the script.

From my seat, it wasn't always a walk in the park either. Melissa was a tough cookie—deeply entrenched in a drama queen mentality. While she was intrigued by this paradoxical idea that she would actually become more empowered by taking responsibility for her own reactivity rather than try to micromanage the rest of the world, it also frightened her to face this because she was trapped in a blame-shame paradigm. In other words, she believed that if she couldn't blame the rest of the world, she'd have to blame herself for her own messes. This would make her feel bad about herself, and she'd already felt as bad as she ever wanted to feel when she was living under the same roof as her mother. Oh no—she'd have none of that again. Thus, in order for Melissa to begin to truly eliminate her drama queen syndrome, she had to come to understand that she could actually throw away the entire concept of blame and replace it with concepts like accountability, choice, and responsibility.

Melissa could certainly be entertaining at times. Hey, I'm only human and it's sometimes fun to hear about stories after the tragic dust has already settled, especially when you can see that no one is worse for the wear as a result. But I also found myself becoming tremendously sad and worried about her. So naturally, I wanted to laugh at some of the insanity she reported. But, at other times, I wanted to shake her back into reality and shout, "Stop making such a big deal out of nothing!" But because Melissa was in such a self-destructive cycle, I often found myself compelled to put my arms around her and hold her until she stopped running on empty and "crying wolf." Well, as it turns out, I didn't actually engulf her with too many hugs since I certainly could never take on the role of replacement mother. But I did embark on a process of hugging her with my words and giving her new ideas for change.

From both my heart and my professional experience, I knew Melissa could become the fully mature and capable young woman I believed she could be, but I also knew that she didn't believe in her own strength. And, her emotional maturity had not caught up with her chronological age. In fact, she was still functioning as a wounded little girl who never got her primary needs for love and affection met by her caregivers. And not only had her cup never been filled up, in her memory banks, she was never even allowed to have a cup to begin with.

I could see very clearly that Melissa's dramatic shenanigans weren't coming from a malicious or intentionally destructive place. She just couldn't help herself. She had no model or framework for how to develop effective coping mechanisms. And she couldn't help but perceive the world as a threatening place in need of constant monitoring for danger. So we had to start at the beginning—that is, from childhood up through to the present and then move quickly into changing her life in the present.

Melissa was the first to admit that she encountered many problems in her childhood and she had no trouble pointing the finger at her mother for all the problems she endured as an adult. But what she failed to recognize was that blaming her childhood for her current problems was never going to do anything to free her from the chains of being a drama queen. Rather she had to learn that regardless of what she endured, it was her job to heal the wounds and put the past to rest. She had to accept that her responses and reactions to life in adulthood were entirely her responsibility and choice.

Once she was able to embrace this concept without shame or blame, she became ready to actually do the work of changing her response style.

The Problem

For starters, Melissa began to identify the triggers to her over-responding from each of the three dominant categories: rejection, loss, and unforeseen changes. Any of these conditions, in whatever shape or form they would show up, could send Melissa into a tizzy.

Melissa's trigger list included:

- not being invited to a party—even when she couldn't attend anyway
- having someone change a plan or time for a get-together
- not being able to get the meal she wanted in a restaurant if the restaurant ran out of the fish special
- misplacing her keys
- spilling a drink on her shirt, even when she's just hanging out at home watching TV
- having a student not like her teaching style
- not being able to answer her cell phone before it got picked up by her voicemail
- having a stranger not respond to her in an elevator when she's said "hello"
- getting an "unexpectedly" high credit card bill in the mail, even though she's the one who made all the purchases
- getting stuck in a traffic jam and arriving late, knowing that she didn't leave enough driving time for even the best of circumstances

The list goes on and on. Melissa had to come to accept that the things that riled her were no different than what most people deal with on a day-to-day basis. These were not exceptional circumstances and certainly not reason to lose any sleep over. This was a very hard lesson for Melissa as she kept trying to convince me that her days were harder than most people's. And she was right, but not because they were legitimately more stressful than your average Joe's experience. They were harder because she experienced daily life more intensely than non-drama queens due to the way she processed daily events. She felt victimized by minor upsets whereas other people were able to take ownership of the events that they were responsible for but not try to control what is outside of their control. Once Melissa grasped this concept, a whole new world opened up for her.

As the process progressed Melissa learned how to use the R.E.A.C.T. assessment on a regular basis. (You'll learn more about this in Chapter Five.) Initially she had to implement this strategy consciously and deliberately, but eventually it became almost an automatic style. This laid the foundation for her to recognize that she actually does have control over how she responds and reacts to life's events.

Then we tackled Melissa's expectations and beliefs about people. Essentially, because of her deprived childhood, lacking in emotional security, nurturance, and self-esteem boosters, Melissa became a very anxious person who didn't trust in her own resources to take care of herself. Plus, to make matters worse, she also unconsciously expected the rest of the world to provide her with the emotional supplies she failed to receive in childhood and to make up for everything she didn't get. And this entitlement continued to keep her stuck in her drama queen syndrome. She truly expected the world to operate smoothly to make up for the rough road she had had as a kid. But the world just doesn't operate that way. And while it was a painful discovery for Melissa to realize that the rest of the world really doesn't care about her hardships, it was also remarkably helpful.

Mind you, I'm certainly not implying that people are heartless or uncaring. In fact, one of the primary reasons we humans desire to be in intimate relationships is because we want people closest to us to be loving and to support us through difficult times. We want to know that we matter to other people in order to feel as if our lives are meaningful. But we simply can't expect *everyone* to care about us or to make up for what our histories lacked. For instance, we certainly can't expect the grocery store checker to give a darn about the childhood roots of our over-reactivity. The checker's job is to scan and bag the groceries—not to provide psychotherapy. So, taking this a step further, if you forget your wallet (because you're so overwhelmed with your life), then while "your story" may be interesting, all the checker really cares about is how you're going to pay for your groceries or how to void the order and get on to the next customer. This is just reality. And Melissa needed to learn that she simply could no longer expect people to have to compensate for whatever deficits she endured.

Next, Melissa learned how to distinguish truly dangerous situations requiring a crisis reaction from those that weren't such a big deal. One of the helpful tools she learned was to ask herself a few questions before getting worked up over nothing. Some of these questions included:

1. If I don't react to this situation right away, what will likely happen?
2. Is there any hidden motive to why I feel compelled to react strongly to this situation, such as a need for attention, insecurity, boredom, fear of being abandoned, or some other emotional need?
3. How will I feel tomorrow if I let this situation slide off my back without much response?

Using this assessment tool, Melissa became better equipped to put some distance between a stimulus and her response. A stimulus could be anything from something as benign as having an orange fall off the display table at the supermarket to having an entire display of oranges tumble down and spread out all over the floor. (Please note: Melissa was not instructed to ever use this tool in an actual life-threatening situation. For example, she would not use this strategy if she were to see a car coming at her head on. Then she should react exactly as her body tells her to by getting the heck out of the way.)

Having just a little bit more time before reacting on automatic pilot helped Melissa handle crisis situations more effectively and allowed her to become less stressed out about trivial matters. Plus, taking a pause and becoming conscious of her initial impulse to overreact also freed up a lot more time and energy so that she could have more fun. For instance, rather than getting all upset over spilling soda on her pants and wasting time being dramatic over it, she could simply go and get a paper towel and blot up the spill or change her pants (if another pair were available).

Like most drama queens, Melissa believed that her feelings directed her actions. What she had a hard time grasping was that feelings don't dictate behavior at all. Rather, our behavior and actions are choices. And our emotions emerge because of how we perceive a situation. In other words, just because someone is angry doesn't mean he has to throw a chair out the window. Instead he could set a boundary and remove himself from whatever situation he finds offensive. But he could also check out his perception of the situation and see whether there could be an alternative way of viewing something, which might then change his anger into some other feeling.

In Melissa's case, because she had become so used to people rejecting and abandoning her, she frequently misperceived people's behavior as a rejection of her even when they weren't being rejecting at all. So if a friend didn't return a call, she would quickly jump to the conclusion that she was getting dumped, even if her friend legitimately forgot to call because she was preoccupied with some other thing going on in her life. And Melissa would frequently become angry and then react with verbal rage, often creating the very situation she feared: that is, her friend would then reject her. Once Melissa realized that her feelings were intimately linked to her perceptions and she came to recognize that she had choices about how to react, she was able to calm down considerably in situations that would normally cause her to overreact.

Next we tackled Melissa's expectations of other people and of herself. When Melissa first came to see me it was clear that she had enormously high expectations of herself and of other people's performance. To make matters even worse, she had little patience and very little tolerance for frustration. She wanted things to be "just right" all the time and she wanted what she wanted right away. Her perfectionist standards actually served as a cover-up for feeling inadequate and unlovable. But once she realized that her self worth was not contingent upon doing everything super well, she made room for accepting "good enough" in many areas of her life and she could save her perfectionist ideals for things that truly mattered. Plus, she no longer needed everyone else to constantly prove that they cared about her. For instance, she discovered that she could create a better learning environment for her students if she wasn't so picky about having all of their chairs perfectly lined up. After all, it was *teaching* that was important to her. And more than anything she didn't want to become like her mother with a military style of relating to her students. And, eventually, she made peace with the idea that all her students wouldn't necessarily think she was the best teacher in the whole world, no matter how hard she would try to endear herself to them. But, that didn't mean that she couldn't win the hearts of the bulk of them.

Melissa was able to continue becoming a happier and easier-going person with far fewer drama queen episodes once she began mastering the "turning chicken shit into chicken salad" philosophy. Remember, this is not a recipe for becoming a Pollyanna or embracing the defense mechanism of denial. But rather, it's a philosophy that encourages us to accept that we cannot change what has already occurred, but we can certainly change how it affects us.

No one would argue that Melissa had a tough childhood and wasn't dealt the best hand of cards from the deck of life. But while we are essentially powerless and unable to make our own choices about our well-being during our youth, as we grow up, the balance shifts. And at some point we become more and more responsible for our behavior and the choices we make. And while we may not start out with the best hand, eventually we learn that we have choices about how to deal with the hand we're dealt *and* that often we can even trade in our cards. And in adulthood we're held accountable by others for our own behavior and the consequences. So while Melissa certainly didn't choose to have the kind of emotionally-deprived and abusive family system she was raised in, it happened and she could either stay stuck feeling like a victim to it (hence the origin of her particular drama queen syndrome) or she could conquer it and make it work for her.

Clearly it was in her best interest to make the most of what she had and find the silver lining in her experience. Hence much of Melissa's work centered around helping her get rid of her old pain and suffering. And she came to realize that while she had convinced herself that she had been debilitated by her childhood experience and consequently reliant on the world to give her what she didn't get, she was actually given a gift in disguise. What she endured had made her *stronger*, not weaker.

Mind you, drama queens who didn't experience deprivation or abuse, but who were indulged and given everything they wanted, also often fail to learn how to tolerate frustration and delay gratification. So while this group may not have the same feelings of having been wounded or deprived, they still suffered consequences from being overly indulged. But this too can be transformed into their strength.

Once Melissa could see the diamond in the rough, she could let go of the emotional baggage stemming from unhealed wounds from her childhood and truly learn to live in the moment and take charge of her happiness. Not only could she implement tools to eliminate anxiety, but she became far less fearful and over-reactive. Most importantly, she learned to distinguish the boundaries defining where she had control and where she didn't. While she'd spent so much time and energy in her life trying to control other people, places, and things, she ultimately learned that she is only responsible for her own feelings, thoughts, and behavior. Of course, that will change to some extent should she ever decide to raise a dependent child. But for the time being, Melissa only has herself to worry about. What a relief. And by actually letting go of trying to control every thing outside of her, she became more energized and empowered.

Melissa also learned the importance and the art of self-care. Because she'd spent so much of her life trying to get her needs met from others, naturally she was more vulnerable to the ups and downs of daily living. She had to learn that most people won't be able to meet her needs most of the time and that it was her job to keep herself healthy, emotionally and physically. Plus, by rearranging her priorities—putting all of her financial resources toward things that would really matter instead of into superficial things—she found that she had a lot more resources to spend on her personal well-being, despite her modest teacher's salary. She even found that she could afford a personal trainer and a massage now and again and spend a little less money on hyped-up hair and skin care products.

Melissa's ultimate challenge was to test out what she'd been learning by applying her new tools within her relationships. Initially she practiced in her friendships (the few she had) and eventually she branched out and made new friends. Her growth didn't stop there, but transferred into her romantic life as well. While she got tripped up a few times by getting sucked back into occasional over-reactivity, she was able to get back on track quickly and more easily and keep making progress. So she re-entered the world of dating with a whole new set of tools and ways of thinking. And, after kissing several frogs, she landed on Paul's lily pad. Last I heard, she and Paul were talking about plans for marriage and she felt secure and grounded in the relationship. (Okay, so they have a little drama now and then—but that's to be expected in any intimate relationship.) Melissa's work life also improved, with her becoming a much more effective teacher than she'd ever imagined she could be and without all the stress and pressure she once placed on herself.

Way to go, Melissa!

Of course, I share all of these details of Melissa's life because I want you to feel inspired and hopeful. If Melissa can make such enormous changes, you can too! So now let's move on to the nuts and bolts of how you can make your own transformation or help along one of your loved ones.

Chapter 4

The Button Pushers
of Over-reactivity

I've already established that the drama queen syndrome can emerge from a whole variety of things, including environmental, temperamental, and/or hereditary factors. And because so many variables can influence how our personality and coping styles develop, it should come as no surprise that each drama queen has a unique profile. But while there are many differences among drama queens, they share several overlapping features as well. In fact, I've found during the course of more than two decades of experience in working with lovable drama queens that this group shares a commonality in the area of what tends to trigger the over-reactivity; that is, the *button pushers*.

But before we move on to understanding the common button pushers and the exercises to neutralize them, we need to address the issue of shame. Why? Because whether you admit it or not, most people don't refer to drama queens in the most flattering of terms. Rather, many people stereotype drama queens as "nuts" and as people who should be avoided at all costs. So in case you haven't already noticed, I often refer to drama queens as *lovable* because I want to destigmatize this label. And, I want you to know that being a drama queen doesn't mean you're crazy and certainly doesn't imply that you're a bad person in any way.

Actually it's highly likely that becoming a drama queen served a very useful purpose in your life at one point—possibly even having had survival value. This is particularly true if your syndrome developed from childhood trauma or mistreatment. But while it may once have had an adaptive function, it probably no longer serves you well. But even if you have not ever thought of yourself as a drama queen and you only came upon this book because a trusted significant other thought it might be a good resource for you, you're probably getting the message by now that you might need to spend some time revising your approach to the world to improve your relationships and overall quality of life.

Because the label of being a drama queen can come with many negative connotations, I simply must emphasize again that I absolutely don't want you to feel trapped underneath a pile of shame. Rather, I want you to embrace who you are with love and acceptance *and* look at your syndrome as something that needs a bit of tweaking.

The key to remember when addressing your drama queen syndrome, or anything that keeps you stuck in anxiety and limits your capacity for tranquility, is that if something no longer serves its original purpose, then it's best to develop new ways of coping. In other words, it's time to learn new tools and to change what no longer works anymore. Of course, that's why you're reading this guidebook!

Even if you bear a borderline resemblance to the emotional vampire types I described at the beginning of the book, you still have reasons for having become who you are. (But that doesn't mean you can use these reasons as excuses any longer.) Your work just may be a little bit harder. So, unless you have evil intent behind your actions or you truly don't care about anyone but yourself, then I want you to feel good about yourself. And, while it's okay to judge your *behavior*, especially since it's wreaking havoc in many, if not all, areas of your life, it's not okay to judge your *being*.

The Button Pushers of Over-reactivity

It is ever so important that you understand that no matter how severe your drama queen syndrome has become, you *are* lovable and most definitely worthy of having the happiness and tranquility you desire and deserve. You're not some alien creature to whom no one should get close. You simply have to recognize that even though your behavior may irritate others (and possibly even yourself), you're still entitled to your fair share of attention and love just like everyone else. You just need to find better ways to get it. And, you just have to lay the foundation for a new way of balancing and approaching the day-to-day ups and downs of life.

So just in case you're having any moments of shame or embarrassment, please take a few deep breaths and say these words aloud:

No matter what I've been dealt with in life to create the person I've become, I deserve to have tranquility and happiness like everyone else. But because I'm now an adult and need to be responsible for my actions, I must commit to making healthy choices about how I react and behave in the present time. And, from here forward, I need to accept that it's my job to make the necessary changes in how I approach my life so that I can have what I deserve. No blame, no shame, just change!

Anytime you find the annoying shame bug buzzing around in your head, swat it a few times by repeating the words above again and again until you start to believe them. Also, by continually reminding yourself that you *are not* a bad person for being a drama queen, you actually open the door to become willing to be more responsible for your own behavior. Hence, you'll increase your capacity to take the steps toward positive changes.

I want this learning experience to be a good one for you and one that feels exciting and challenging—not one where you feel like you're being dragged naked across coarse sandpaper. Ouch—that would not be good! The last thing you need is to feel as though you're being judged or ridiculed for your over-sensitivity and ultimate over-reactivity. I'm sure you've had just about enough of those negative responses toward you. Plus, as we continue on, keep in mind that you need to set your own pace

71

The Problem

and remember that *you* are in charge of making the choices about what you want to discover and change. If something doesn't fit or make sense to you, then feel free to chuck it. And whatever you do, don't overwhelm yourself by taking on more than you can chew. You've lived as a drama queen for some time already, so taking a little extra time to process your discoveries and learn new responses isn't going to kill you. This material and guidance is meant to soothe and calm you, not to push your buttons. Good, now we can move on to understanding exactly what gets you riled up.

Button Pushers

Drama queens can be triggered into over-reactivity by just about anything—a person, a place, or a situation—depending upon the personal meaning the stimulus has for them. In severe cases where someone suffers from a condition called post-traumatic stress disorder (also known as PTSD), the triggers are often things that remind the person of a real trauma. By the way, "real trauma" is any situation or event where a person is exposed to something outside the realm of normal human experience such as witnessing a murder, being trapped in a burning building, or being raped. But most drama queens don't fit the full clinical picture of PTSD even though at one point in their lives they may have experienced major traumas. And also, all people who experience life-death trauma don't all end up with PTSD or even the drama queen syndrome. "How can that be?" you might ask. Again, people process things differently. Some people are equipped with better or different resources than others or they simply have a stronger constitution and more innate resiliency from the get-go. (For more on PTSD, please refer to the final chapter.)

While drama queens can be very convincing that what they're reacting to is truly a crisis once their buttons have been pushed, most of the time they're simply responding to perceived or imagined danger. While some do this consciously with the aim of getting attention, others aren't even aware that they're creating a monster out of a tiny mouse. Unknowingly, they're embellishing a situation in their minds—that is, they become highly fearful of a consequence that's *unlikely* to occur.

For a drama queen, even something as simple as breaking a nail can be grounds for over-reactivity because she may believe that without perfect nails (whatever her definition of that might be) she will lose her chances of meeting the lover of her dreams. She may actually go so far as to believe that she is unattractive and will never be able to find anyone who will love her, let alone find her ideal mate. While this may sound insane to people who don't know what it's like to be afflicted with drama queen syndrome, for the drama queen, this is a real crisis because the *imagined* consequences of this unforeseen event are catastrophic.

Teresa, a thirty-year-old advertising executive, is a great example of someone who couldn't help but perceive minor events as potentially catastrophic. No matter how hard she tried (before she embarked on a journey to tackle her drama queen syndrome), she would inevitably project the worst possible outcome for every event, regardless of the significance of the event. For Teresa, a raindrop falling on her shirt or an unexpected line at the bank could trigger as much anxiety as actually having a potentially fatal car accident because, in her mind, the end result would be death. I know this may sound strange to those of you who are reading this in order to help a drama queen and not because you identify yourself having the syndrome. But to drama queens, this makes perfect sense because they have triggers that cause a sequence of "what ifs?" In other words, they perceive an event and, without even realizing it, they start processing the worst possible outcome. "If this happens, then this will happen, which will cause this, and then wow, I'm doomed," is an example of the sequence. The drama queen is simply responding as though the whole sequence has already occurred and her goal is to prevent disaster.

Here's an example of how Teresa would work herself up into a tizzy, regardless of how benign a situation would appear to the average person.

The Problem

Using the alphabet as a metaphor, let's say Z represents actual disaster, such as death, total annihilation, and/or incapacitation. Each letter of the alphabet after A represents something continually more catastrophic. I won't bore you with all twenty-six letters in the alphabet of "what ifs" but here is an example of the sequence using a few of the letters.

Teresa wakes up and discovers that she set the timer on her coffee-maker to 6:30 p.m. instead of a.m. (event A). A non-drama queen would say "Oops" and then press the "on" button, hit the shower, and then come back to pour herself a cup of java. But this wasn't the case for Teresa. She would then jump to "now I'm going to be late for work" (somewhere about a D) to "If I'm late to work, my boss will be mad at me" (about a G) to "I'm such an idiot, why can't I do anything right" (about a J) to "I deserve to be fired" (about an M) to "Actually, I'm sure I'll get fired" (about a P) to "Holy shit. That means I'll be homeless by next week because I won't get a pay check and I have nothing in my savings account" (definitely a catastrophic event somewhere in the X, Y, or Z range).

Teresa's response to incorrectly setting the coffee timer wouldn't even stop at simply playing the whole catastrophic tape in her head. She would then take it a step further and start engaging other people in her perceived disaster. For instance, she might go so far as to actually call friends and family and tell them that she's about to lose her job. Of course, she wouldn't get fired, but she might have spent a whole day in spiraling anxiety about something she completely drummed up in her own mind. Then not only would she have to contend with her own feelings of embarrassment and regret for having created such a huge deal out of something small, but she would also have to calm everyone else down around her whom she had brought into her mind-screwing tizzy.

Poor Teresa—what a burden to have to bear. And all because she simply made an inconsequential mistake. What's even worse, she only drank decaf so she wasn't even waiting for a caffeine jolt! Nevertheless, as silly as this may sound, and even Teresa herself would look back at this and laugh, this had become a common way for her to respond to even the most benign events. (Imagine how she would have reacted had she *actually* gotten fired.)

Teresa's buttons, like those of many drama queens, were very easily pushed. For Teresa it really didn't matter whether she started from A (totally benign, neutral event), M (possibly an event that could lead to danger), or Y (almost certain that without crisis intervention catastrophe would occur), her behavior (highly reactive) would almost always signify that she'd perceived the situation to ultimately lead to a level Z. She was constantly plagued by anticipating disaster and trying to control her future without ever really living in the present and dealing with minor upsets appropriately. Thankfully, she sought help and was able to learn how to accurately distinguish between imagined danger and real danger.

So what are the common button pushers? Of course, I don't have the definitive answer for you since each of us is a unique being with a unique history and biological blueprint. But from my experience, both personally and professionally, I've found there to be three major triggers: loss, rejection, and/or unforeseen changes. Looking back at Teresa for a moment you can see that all three of these are often present at the same time: loss (the threat of losing her job), rejection (she rejected herself because of a mistake and she feared rejection from her boss), and unforeseen changes—she hadn't anticipated not getting her coffee on time.

Here are some examples of the various things in day-to-day life from each of these categories. Though keep in mind that you could probably make a case for each item to fit into all the categories depending on your own perceptual twists (a very clever skill of drama queens), but for simplicity's sake I've separated them into three categories.

Loss (fear of loss or actual loss)

Losses come in as many varieties as there are models and makes of automobiles. They can be extremely traumatic such as the loss of your home due to a fire or the death of a loved one to cancer; or they can be minor and irritating like losing your keys (but finding them), or dropping a penny in a muddy puddle and not being able to find it (or not wanting to waste the time). Losses can come in the form of real events or in one's imagination. The same loss might be perceived as something positive in one context (like losing ten pounds, if you're purposely attempting a weight-loss program) or as something negative in a different context (like losing ten pounds because of stress when you're already underweight).

The impact of any one loss varies for each individual. Some losses that may seem huge to one person may not have much of an impact on another because of the context of the loss. For instance, Jenny and Lucy lived together for four years and Jenny loved their relationship, but Lucy felt smothered and spent two of the four years contemplating how she was going to break up with Jenny. Lucy wasn't a great communicator in the best of situations and she had even more difficulty communicating her feelings to Jenny because Jenny never seemed able to handle any kind of critical feedback. Hence, Lucy never actually came right out and expressed to Jenny just how bad she felt about their relationship. And one day, she came home from the work and announced to Jenny that she was moving out.

While it certainly would have been better for Lucy to learn how to communicate to Jenny along the way, she was just too afraid of how Jenny would react. When she finally did break the news to Jenny that she had had it with their relationship, Jenny just about lost her mind completely. She became so depressed and anxious that she couldn't eat, sleep, or concentrate. For Jenny the loss was akin to being told that she had a terminal illness with only six more months to live. For Lucy the ending of the relationship was a relief and a time to spread her wings and experience her freedom.

Of course, Jenny might have been spared some of her shock and devastation had Lucy been letting her know more openly along the way of her discontent. But, I'm not so sure she would have handled it much better given the extent to which she was threatened by fear of loss. And because she was so easily triggered in this area, her relationship never really rested on a solid foundation. In fact, it may have even been doomed from the get-go.

Mind you, neither Jenny nor Lucy was a bad or malicious person. Rather, they were both lovely women, but they simply weren't compatible. Plus, they had very different needs and expectations for a relationship. Sadly, for many months following the break-up Jenny couldn't see that she really wasn't getting her needs met from the relationship either. After all, Lucy wasn't able to be emotionally present. But because she couldn't see this reality at first, the loss was far more devastating and intense for her than it was for Lucy.

Clearly, going through a break-up can be very hard on most people. And, having a tough time dealing with a break-up doesn't make one a drama queen. But the level of Jenny's despair suggested that, while she'd never thought of herself as a drama queen, she definitely qualified as one. In fact, in many areas of her life, the threat of loss or a encountering a real loss would cause Jenny to erupt into hysteria. Gratefully, Jenny eventually learned to accept that Lucy had an especially hard time communicating with her because she felt she was constantly walking on eggshells and didn't want to deal with Jenny's over-reactivity anymore.

Most everyone deals with losses on an ongoing basis, though usually not relating to large issues, such as break-ups, illness, or a disaster—at least not very often. But there is a big difference between those who suffer from the drama queen syndrome and those who do not. Non-drama queens don't pay any attention to trivial losses because they experience these mini-losses as par for the course in daily living—that is, as nothing to get riled up over. In contrast, for drama queens, a loss, however small, can be very upsetting and trigger a vicious cycle of fearing further loss. They can't distinguish what warrants a fight-or-flight reaction, from what just needs to be dealt with calmly and thoughtfully.

While I certainly can't create a comprehensive list of every conceivable loss that someone might experience, here are a few examples of things you might relate to. Also, while I've identified the component of the loss, you may see another element I haven't identified. For instance, you might lose a wallet with $50.00 and see this as primarily a "loss of time" more than a "loss of money" because your credit cards would have to be canceled and replaced. And then, on top of that, you'd have to spend time at the Department of Motor Vehicles to get a new driver's license. But if you lose your wallet you may not key into those issues at all, but instead become triggered by what you believe was a "stupid" mistake and now you've lost the little bit of self-esteem you've been hanging onto. You might not care at all about the loss of money or the inconvenience to your schedule. Someone else might become plagued with a sense of loss in all of these areas, and get overwhelmed. So keep these perceptual differences in mind and just use this list as something that prompts you to think about losses in your life that serve as button pushers:

- receiving a parking or speeding ticket (or any loss of money)
- running late to a meeting (or any loss of time)
- getting a promotion (any loss of familiarity of previous position)
- bouncing a check (a loss of good credit or a financial embarrassment)
- throwing out an item of clothing and then finding that you had the perfect event to wear it to (such as a Halloween party) but you no longer have it (the loss of something now perceived as valuable)
- finding your lunch leftovers from two days ago spoiled in the fridge (a loss of money and of a meal you looked forward to)
- getting a cold or the flu (a loss of being able to deal with daily responsibilities, loss of time and energy, etc.)
- having your child come down with a cold or flu and having to leave work early to pick her up from school (the loss of being able to complete a daily to-do-list)

- forgetting to take the trash out on time for pick-up (the loss of space for more trash)

Yes, some of the items listed seem completely trivial, especially if you're a low-level drama queen or someone who is reading this in order to better understand a significant other. But, believe me, any one of these items can activate a drama queen's buttons and send him or her into a tailspin. For instance, some people might see finding leftovers in a rotted state in their fridge to be a blessing in disguise. They might think, "Thanks goodness this stuff can't be eaten. I wasn't really in the mood for meatloaf again, but I wouldn't have wanted to see it go to waste. Now I can have what I really want—a BLT sandwich." A drama queen, however, would have a very different reaction if his loss-buttons got pushed. He might respond more like this: "I can't believe I let this go to waste. There are starving children all over the world and here I am throwing out food I should have eaten! I don't deserve to have anything to eat for the rest of the day."

Obviously if you only had $5.00 left to your name and you had spent it on a sandwich, you might get upset if you had purposely saved half to eat at a later time and then discovered it had spoiled because your electricity had been turned off before you had a chance to eat your leftovers. That might have been your last meal for a while. Of course, you'd be alarmed. But more than likely, this would not be the case and there would be no real loss, certainly not one that would warrant full-fledged hysteria.

Rejection

This is a big one for drama queens. Clearly, there are the obvious rejections that are often paired with a loss such as someone breaking up with you, or being passed over for a promotion that you were certain you would get. But some rejections aren't necessarily tied to anything that would lead to emotional pain or suffering. In fact, some rejections actually lead to a gain or positive experience. Yet drama queens often put all rejections into the same pile and react to them as though they signify the end of the world.

For instance, Antoinette, a twenty-six-year-old ballet dancer, responded to all rejections with the same reaction: assault on her self-esteem. And more often than not, rejections of all varieties would trigger in her a deep fear of abandonment. Even though she was a full-fledged adult who had been supporting herself financially for over eight years, she responded to the world as though she were still a little girl under threat of being sent away to an orphanage if she misbehaved. (Sadly, her mother and father had threatened to get rid of her on a regular basis.)

Once when Antoinette was about twenty-four years old, she was summoned for jury duty. And even though she was in the middle of rehearsing for one of her biggest performances in the history of her dancing career and would clearly be incredibly burdened if she were selected for a trial, she was devastated when she wasn't picked to sit on the jury. Basically, she was rejected by the defense without any explanation. Rather than being relieved that her time for rehearsal would now be uninterrupted, she fell into a *shame hole*—that is, a psychological space where we perceive ourselves as unworthy of living or, at best, defective in our core being. Essentially, Antoinette personalized the rejection and thought that something was wrong with her because she wasn't selected.

Whereas many people would be thrilled to get a free pass from jury duty, Antoinette started crying in the courthouse and wasn't able to sleep for days. Like so many drama queens, Antoinette linked pain to all rejections. She couldn't understand that one could have many different emotional reactions to being rejected, depending on the context. The reality is that there might have been ten reasons for not being considered right for a jury on a particular case, not one of which having anything to do with Antoinette's value as a person. But until she recognized that the act of being rejected didn't have to be a button pusher, she couldn't help but feel personally wounded.

The Button Pushers of Over-reactivity

Sounds bleak, doesn't it? But rest assured, Antoinette's tale has a positive ending. A couple of years later, she got called for jury duty again. But this time she'd already gotten a handle on her drama queen syndrome and she no longer linked all rejections with painful emotions or shame holes. And guess what? She was chosen to sit on the jury for a complicated case. But was she happy about it? Not at all. If fact, she was rather pissed off because she was actually hoping to be rejected! But she didn't go into a tailspin over it. She just accepted that it was her duty as a citizen and she understood she would have to make the best of it.

Whether we like it or not, we all experience rejections, big and small, across our life spans. Certainly, some people experience far fewer rejections than the rest of us because they have more money, are more attractive, or have other qualities that translate into more power. But by and large, rejection is as much a part of how the world operates as is the changing of the seasons. But for drama queens who believe that they're self-worth is contingent upon being wanted and desired by everyone, all of the time, then anything less than full-fledged acceptance becomes a stab in the heart and often leads to over-reactivity.

Jack, a thirty-five-year-old bank teller, constantly sought everyone's approval. Jack grew up in a large family as the middle child of five kids (three boys and two girls). Though his parents in no way mistreated him and he wasn't teased by his siblings any more than any of the others were, he was a very sensitive child and took things to heart more than the average child. He did just about everything he could to avoid getting in trouble by following all of the household rules and always offering to lend an extra helping hand to members of his family. He couldn't stand anyone being upset with him, particularly his mother who tended to get easily annoyed and would raise her voice whenever she got irritated.

Also, probably of most significance to how Jack developed such a high need for approval and sensitivity toward rejection was that, unlike the siblings who each seemed to have a unique quality his parents admired, Jack didn't think he possessed anything that made him stand out as special.

The Problem

For instance, his younger sister was a brilliant musician, and his younger brother and older sister were gifted athletes. His older brother was the brainy one. Jack, on the other hand, was not very good at any one thing, at least that's what it might have seemed like to the casual observer. Mind you, although his family didn't take notice of any one special quality of Jack's, he was loved and well cared for. Nevertheless, Jack grew up with a big hole in his self-esteem, leaving him ripe for developing the drama queen syndrome.

As it turns out, however, Jack did possess a very valuable talent. Though not obviously perceived by others as an actual gift, Jack had a very unique capacity for prompting and encouraging people to share things about themselves that they might not ordinarily disclose. When not activated by the rejection button, he could be extremely charming, engaging, and endearing. He would be the guy everyone would want to have as a party host. As long as he got people to smile and engage with him, he was happy and at ease. Sure, he would embellish a bit here and there to get a laugh or some extra attention, but he wouldn't do the kinds of things drama queens often do that drive people away.

By adulthood, Jack's knack for facilitating openness in others became the quality he valued most. And as a result, he felt compelled to befriend everyone. But expecting to be able to appeal to everyone and become everyone's best buddy is a recipe for disappointment and disaster, not to mention a complete set-up for feeling personally rejected. No doubt, Jack's amicable personality certainly won the hearts of many acquaintances, and he had many friends. But every now and again he'd encounter someone who would perceive him in a negative light and actually experience his kindness as weakness or as a form of sucking up. Plus, in his day-to-day activities he would encounter people who would be in a bad mood or preoccupied with something or inwardly focused. If Jack had made any effort at all to make contact with these people and he didn't get the desired response of some sort of endearment, he would freak out, sometimes becoming so irate as though someone had set out personally to offend him.

The Button Pushers of Over-reactivity

As time went on, Jack became increasingly sensitive to rejection. He would personalize everything. At times he almost appeared paranoid, believing that people were talking about him behind his back. Things really got bad at his job where he had to work side-by-side with another teller who found Jack to be overbearing and too needy. And the more Jack felt disliked, the more compelled he felt to get in someone's face. He wasn't trying to annoy others. Quite the contrary. He was on a constant mission to win favor in other people's eyes. But some people found him to be annoying and he couldn't handle it.

Despite his good intentions, Jack had no clue that the very gift of making people feel comfortable could also be a curse with some people. And he truly needed to develop a thicker skin. It was great that he could be so endearing, but he also needed to learn to let some things just roll off his back. He had to come to accept that he truly didn't *need* everyone's approval to be okay in the world. He could get by with a little less and not make such a big deal out of rejections. Up until he learned how to tame his drama queen syndrome, he wasn't even able to date. He was so intimidated and afraid he'd be rejected that he never took any risks to attempt an intimate relationship. Fortunately, once he recognized the roots of his over-reactivity, he was able to reframe rejections as a regular part of life and something that wouldn't kill him.

One of the things that make rejection become such a big trigger for drama queens is that they often mistake rejection as a feeling, and a negative one at that. In other words, people will often say "I feel rejected." But in actuality, rejection is an event or action and it would be more accurate to say "I have been rejected by (fill in the blank)" and then name the feeling attached to the event. Thus, the act of being rejected doesn't determine how one will feel about the rejection. One could just as easily feel glad about being rejected as feeling sad or hurt. (You'll learn more about feelings in Chapter Seven.)

Also once we recognize that we, too, continuously reject people, places, and things—usually not based on anything specific or personal— we can more easily put rejection in perspective. For instance, when we go to the supermarket and pick a bunch of apples out of a pile of hundreds to choose from, we're not leaving the others behind because they're rotten. Sometimes it's just random or based on a particular preference, not because there is something objectively *bad* about the thing we're not choosing. For instance, you might like your apples to be very red and firm whereas someone else might prefer apples that are green and a little overly ripened. I know it's harder when dealing with human emotion, but it's still important to put rejections in perspective.

For a moment, stop and think about your day-to-day routines and how often you commit acts of rejection. For instance, I can think of several things I rejected while writing this chapter:

- I didn't take a phone call from a friend, and instead let the call go to voicemail.
- I rejected a thought directing me to pay some bills before my next therapy session with a client.
- I declined an invitation to have lunch with a colleague who was also on a break (in between therapy sessions).
- I threw out my hot tea because I'd let it sit too long and it got cold and too strong for my taste buds.

Of course, it would be silly to consider the feelings of my cup of tea since I'm pretty sure tea doesn't have the capacity to experience emotions. But the other examples involve people. So if my friend found out I dismissed her call or if my colleague (whose invitation to have lunch, I declined) was sensitive to rejection, then it's possible that I may have inadvertently hurt their feelings through my action of rejection. But the reality is that I wasn't actively rejecting anyone and I wasn't rejecting myself by delaying my bill paying. All I was doing was staying focused on my writing because I was having a good flow and didn't want to be interrupted. So you see, by putting rejections in a context, more often than not, they are very meaningless.

The Button Pushers of Over-reactivity

Clearly, some rejections are highly personal and would most likely cause hurt feelings in anyone. For instance, no doubt it would probably be very painful if the person you're madly in love with looks you in the eye and says he doesn't find you attractive anymore and/or doesn't think you're smart. Or worse yet, your spouse tells you she's in love with someone else and is going to leave you. But even these kinds of rejections are not a statement about someone's value in general, just in the eyes of the particular person doing the rejecting. Far too often, drama queens experience the same level of devastation whether the rejection is benign or impersonal (as in not having your business card selected out of a fishbowl to get a free drink at your favorite coffeehouse) or whether the rejection is a personal and specific statement about you (as in having a best friend tell you she thinks you're unreliable and no longer wants to make any more plans to spend time together).

To complicate matters even more, sometimes drama queens perceive a rejection when one hasn't even occurred. For instance, you may not receive an invitation to your good friend's Halloween party one year. And even though you've been invited to the same annual party for the past six consecutive years, you automatically assume that you've done something wrong in the friendship and you're being punished through a rejection. But in fact, there was simply an e-mail or snail mail glitch. But drama queens don't usually start out with neutral assumptions. Rather, they jump to irrational conclusions, especially when involving a potential scenario of rejection.

To summarize, the keys to keep in mind when understanding rejection are:

- Rejection is not a feeling, but rather an action.
- Most rejections are not personal or intentional.
- Even for those rejections that cut to the core, almost all personal rejections are more about the person doing the rejecting than about the objective truth about you.

- Even for those few rejections that may actually target something about you that is a problem, they're still statements about your behavior, not your inner being. And, we can all change behavior, if we so desire.

Now, if you're someone with really low self-esteem or someone who became a drama queen because of some traumatic environmental or genetic influence, these ideas about rejection may be hard to swallow. But, even so, you still needn't experience rejection as a tragedy or as signifying the end of the world. For instance, maybe you lost a leg in a car accident and now you may feel that you're no longer a "physically" whole human. All I can do is attempt to empathize with how awful it must be to have had such trauma and result. And no doubt, because we live in a world filled with prejudice and judgment, I would imagine that someone in this position would also experience a tremendous amount of rejection from others. But while I don't have any personal experience to relate to in this regard, I have witnessed people who have even been able to turn this kind of adversity into strength and not be rattled by the inevitable foolish behavior of insensitive others.

I know this is a dark example, but I really want to drive home the message that even in situations where someone does become physically compromised due to tragedy or starts out that way, these situations do not determine someone's worthiness. And despite a flow of ongoing rejection, one can choose how to react. Thankfully, most of us won't ever have to endure such trauma, but it's good to use this as a reminder of what constitutes *true* tragedy versus that which is embellished in our minds.

Below is a list of some examples of common rejections that are often perceived by drama queens to be "near tragic" when in fact these events don't objectively determine a negative outcome. As you read through these examples, also try to think about the ways in which you've allowed the action of rejection to lead to over-reactivity. If you don't like what

The Button Pushers of Over-reactivity

you discover or you think it's silly, don't sentence yourself to a lifelong imprisonment of shame. Instead, think of ways you can change your response. Also please note that these are just random, and not exhaustive, examples of scenarios involving themes of rejection. An exhaustive list would be impossible.

Some of the scenarios listed below imply a rejection that's personal in nature; others are random and non-specific but can easily be interpreted as something about you, if you're prone to being a drama queen. And just for fun, try to imagine yourself in these scenarios even if you've never experienced the context as I describe it and see what you think each scenario depicts: either something "personal" or "impersonal." Keep in mind there is no right or wrong answer. Also, for those scenarios you think are "personal," try to rethink these and "de-personalize" the meaning or intention behind these events. For significant others, please use this list as a tool to increase compassion and appreciation for just how much a rejection (personal or impersonal) can serve as a button pusher for a drama queen. (I've put my own description of the level of "personalness" in parentheses.)

- Your car breaks down. You then call a towing service, but no one at the tow yard is available to help you (completely impersonal).
- You're driving on the freeway, you put on your signal to change lanes, and a driver in the car next to you won't allow you to merge (completely impersonal since he probably isn't even paying attention, unless you had just cut someone off and he is now seeking revenge).
- You go to a restaurant, wait for a table, and a then a VIP gets seated before you do, even though you've been waiting longer (very slightly personal but only because you're not known to the establishment, and certainly doesn't have anything to do with your objective worthiness as a person).

- Your best friend fails to show up for your lunch date and she doesn't call right away (most likely, highly impersonal. Something probably happened on her way to meet you or she just forgot to put it in her calendar).

- You get laid off from your job and two of your coworkers with the same job description get to stay on the job (somewhat personal, but certainly not a statement about your employability and may not even have much to do with you at all. It may be that your boss prefers the personality styles of the other coworkers, or he drew names out of a hat, etc.).

- Your boss fires you for poor work performance, showing up late, and gossiping with coworkers (highly personal, but still not about who you are as a person, but rather a warning that you should probably work on improving your behavior if you want to be employable in the future).

- You get stood up by a date by someone whom you chatted with online, but had never met in person (barely personal—people don't show up for dates for all kinds of reasons having nothing to do with the person they're supposed to meet—they could get cold feet, feel inadequate, have gotten back together with a former partner, changed their minds, etc.).

- Your spouse of the past ten years fails to show up for your anniversary dinner because you had a horrific fight the night before and he's punishing you (personal, but actually more about him because he doesn't have the manners or the maturity to at least tell you he's calling the dinner off before you end up showing up to an empty table for two).

Unforeseen Changes

Losses and rejections also usually involve unforeseen changes, but there are countless other changes that don't involve either loss or rejection. And very often unforeseen changes are considered positive events by most everyone, yet they can also lead to a drama queen reaction. For drama queens, even changes they anticipate and prepare for can cause stress and distress, but the ones that weren't foreshadowed can be especially alarming. And if these events are negative in nature, then look out!

Rosy's mother, Carmela, was very controlling and extremely uncomfortable in unpredictable situations. Her home was always spotless, never a glass left on a counter, all the bath towels perfectly hung, and countertops spotless. One might think she suffered from obsessive-compulsive disorder (OCD), but I can't be certain since I never met her in person. According to Rosy, despite her mother's rigidity, she actually functioned fairly well, holding down a job and managing to give the appearance of leading a relatively normal life. At best, I can speculate that Carmela had a mild case of OCD and was able to keep it under wraps by maintaining a stable and orderly environment.

When Rosy came to see me in therapy it was clear that she managed to escape her dreaded fear that she would become just like her mother. While she had certainly adopted many of her mother's characteristics, they were all of a lesser degree. She was nowhere near as controlling as her mother had been. And, unlike her mother who kept the same routine pretty much every day of her life, Rosy had been trying new things and actively engaging in her life.

Sadly, while Rosy continually pushed herself to expand her horizons and not emulate her mother's life, she often wasn't able to really enjoy her adventures because she would inevitably encounter unforeseen events the more she experimented with new things. And such disruptions would freak her out because she'd never learned how to effectively handle life's curve balls. She certainly didn't learn good coping skills from her mother, and she didn't have any other significant role models since her dad had disappeared when she was three. So, whenever things didn't go smoothly—even something as small as missing a turnoff on the freeway—she'd unravel.

The Problem

Even something that would generally be considered a highly positive experience could create high anxiety for Rosy. In fact, shortly before she entered therapy she had received an unexpected promotion and salary increase. Yes—even getting more money in her pocket created stress and resulted in drama queen behavior. She found herself worrying endlessly about what to do with the money and was afraid she'd make a bad decision. She ruminated about whether to pay off her credit card debt or whether to take the trip to Hawaii she'd always dreamed about. When she decided on lowering her credit card debt, she then overwhelmed herself thinking about which card to pay off and how much to pay. She became so wound up she took a week off from work, which almost cost her the promotion. Thankfully, she knew she had to get a grip. Eventually, she welcomed the idea that she no longer had to live her life as an over-reactor and came to accept that unforeseen changes happen all the time.

For significant others, this may seem ludicrous. But trust me, for a drama queen almost anything unexpected can rock his boat and create a fear of capsizing. So be patient and again try to understand this phenomenon without judgment. Later on, you'll learn how to maintain healthy boundaries and not get sucked into the drama queen vacuum. And drama queens, don't worry. My approach is always loving, never harsh or punitive!

While this is probably already obvious to you, just to make sure, here's some examples of unforeseen changes that can activate the drama queen syndrome. Just as with losses and rejections, please read these and also try to think of changes in your life that create instability. You may even discover that you find certain themes. In other words, you're more activated by changes to your time schedule than to fluctuations in your bank account. Or you get far more riled up by weather changes than by unexpected traffic jams. Or you can handle real crises (like a near-fatal car accident) but you become easily flabbergasted and anxious if your child misses one homework assignment while in the second grade.

Here are some examples of common unforeseen changes that can ignite the drama queen fuse:

- being asked to work late one evening when you already have plans
- not being able to fall asleep at your usual bedtime and waking up late the next morning (even when it's on a day when you don't have anywhere particular you have to be)
- having a friend request a change in meeting time or location and you feel you can't say "no" even though it's an inconvenience to you
- planning a day of outdoor activity and then watching the raindrops fall, screwing all up all your plans
- arriving at the movie theater and finding that the show you expected to see has been sold out
- having your child or someone else you love get sick (nothing serious) and you have to re-juggle your schedule to take care of him or her
- going to the grocery store to buy fresh peaches for the fresh peach pie you're planning to make for your dinner guests only to find that the fruit is too hard and not even close to ripe and you will have to improvise and make something else
- getting a parking ticket because you failed to read the fine print on the sign (granted, you could get upset with yourself and go into a drama queen spiral since you probably could have prevented this had you read the sign. But you didn't, so you got a ticket. But does that really have to be something you go nuts over? I think not. But I know it's tempting to find an excuse to berate yourself, if you're that kind of drama queen. But let me assure you, you don't have to anymore).

Exercise

Hopefully the above descriptions and examples help clarify all the ways in which drama queens can get triggered. But before we move on to The Solution section of the book, please take a few minutes and try to make the information in this chapter personally meaningful and useful to you. You can do this any way that works for you. In case you need some guidance, try the following exercise. Keep in mind that the purpose of this exercise is simply to reflect on your behavior and help you make sense of your drama queen syndrome. Remember, the more awareness we have about ourselves (gleaned through a curious lens as opposed to one of blame or shame), the more we cultivate our capacity to make the changes required to become mellower.

Make a list of your own triggers. Think of things on the entire spectrum from small to big and include losses, rejections, and unforeseen changes. You might even rate each item on your list using a scale of 1–10 with 1 indicating the most mild of triggering power and 10 indicating that you're basically screwed—that is, no matter what you've attempted to do to minimize your reactivity up until this point, you always end up in a full-blown drama queen reaction. In doing this exercise, consider all areas of your life, including relationships (friendships, family relationships, parent-child relationships, workplace relationships), work/career, events, time, space, energy, whatever you think is relevant to you.

Most important, don't judge what you discover even if it seems trivial to you now when you're not in a drama queen state. And don't worry about classifying your items into the right categories of losses, rejections, or unforeseen changes. I just used these categories because that's how my brain operates and organizes things. Feel free to use your own distinguishing categories or eliminate them altogether. You could do this in some kind of chronological order from childhood through the present, listing all the memories you have of overreacting to things (or having been told by someone else that you overreacted). Or you could simply free-write whatever associations come to mind.

Now onward to some solutions!

PART II

The Solutions

Chapter 5

Hiking the Real Mountains, Sliding over the Molehills

I'm sure you don't need me to remind you that life isn't always a bowl of cherries, a bed of roses, or a walk in the park. You might get sick with a bad flu, miss a deadline at work because of a family emergency, or realize you forgot your mother's birthday and then feel horribly guilty for hurting her feelings. You might injure yourself while doing a sport and then not be able to attend an annual party you were looking forward to. Or you might come home one day and discover that your cat turned your favorite and very expensive down comforter into his litter box because you accidentally locked him in your bedroom while you were rushing off to work that morning. The unexpected bumps in the road of life are endless, sometimes taking you off your path completely, and at other times, just leading you astray for a short while.

Because of these inevitable pitfalls of life, you have to be constantly vigilant and prepared for the unexpected. Right? Well, actually, that's not exactly true. In fact, contrary to popular drama-queen thinking, you don't really need to be on red alert at all. Rather you can sit back, relax, and trust in your body's built-in reflexive capacity to deal with crisis or danger when it is truly present. But as you well know, drama queens have trouble believing this reality. But before launching into how to distinguish the real mountains from the molehills using the R.E.A.C.T tool, let me try to alleviate some of your skepticism and fear about what you can expect by making your transformation.

Common Drama Queen Fears

It's never easy to make permanent and lasting changes in our reactions and behavior. And even when we believe that changing how we think and act is in our best interest and we have the desire and motivation, we still tend to be resistant to changing our ways. And particularly in times of stress or uncertainty, we're bound to drop back into old standby, familiar styles of reacting. Plus, it's even harder to make effective changes if we remain stuck in certain beliefs about things that aren't actually true. Remember when people believed the Earth was flat? Do you think the average person got excited about the idea of a trip *around* the world? I doubt it. Why? Because people were too darn afraid they'd fall off the edge of the world and they didn't have an alternative to give them comfort that this wouldn't happen. Fortunately, there were a few adventurous explorers who set out to test the waters (no pun intended). But, let's face it. Those who challenge popular thinking are in the minority. Most people tend to maintain the status quo and not rock the boat. So don't feel bad if you're skeptical about being able to actually become someone who can live in the moment and not be so reactive. But please don't rule this out as an impossible challenge before trying.

Now let's examine the three most common fears that might be holding you back from diving into the transformation process. And, don't be surprised if you resonate with all three of these fears.

1. I won't be able to assess real danger and react to it appropriately if I live in the moment.
2. I'll become a Pollyanna type who lives in denial.
3. I'll lose my capacity to experience the full range of emotions.

Let's start with #1. In case you fear that you won't be able to assess real danger if you drop your guard and vigilance to danger, you can rest assured. You won't. Whether you're aware of this or not, we are all equipped with an inherent tool to keep ourselves alive. In fact, unless my information is outdated, one cannot even commit suicide without the aid of something that renders this survival mechanism ineffective. (Thank goodness for that gift, since life can sometimes get rather ugly for some of us now and again. And far too many drama queens in the throes of a depression have hurt themselves on a whim, sometimes to the point of no return.) In other words, you are already pre-programmed with a capacity for fight, flight, or freeze (f-f-f) should danger arise. So even though I'm advocating for you to learn how to chill out or help someone you love lighten up, none of the tools in this book can mess with your inherent capacity to instinctively respond to true danger. Also, all the tools in this book are meant for times when you're overreacting, not for times of real danger or crisis.

Concerning #2, if you fear that you might become a Pollyanna-type person who lives with her head in the sand, never even noticing when something is definitely wrong, you can also rest assured. Remember you're on the other end of the continuum. So you've got a very long way to go before you could ever be confused with an under-reactor or someone who practices too much denial. This just isn't going to happen. But the good news is that even if it were possible to do a 180, everything in this book is aimed at putting you in the driver's seat of your reactions. So this isn't going to just happen to you; you'd have to *decide* to steer yourself down Denial Lane.

Concerning fear #3, many drama queens tell me they like the way it feels to have very strong reactions to things even though they often don't like the consequences. Hence, they fear that they'll lose their capacity to feel their emotions deeply and intensely and worry that they might become like one of those walking zombies portrayed in one of those really bad horror flicks. But again, no worries. You'll soon learn that you have far more power over your emotions than you might have been taught. And hence, if you want to sob up a storm at your daughter's wedding, or you want to wallow in your misery should you discover that your loser husband has been cheating on you, you may if you choose.

So, if you're plagued by any or all of these fears, make a vow right now to let these unnecessary worries go. Essentially, all I want for you—and hope that by now, you also want for yourself—is to be able to help you lessen your tendency to overreact when there really isn't anything tragic going on. And in doing so, you can lighten up and finally let go and go with the flow. Now we can dive into learning how to assess true danger.

Assessing True Danger

Clearly, many situations in life require an f-f-f response, some devastating, some not too bad. Basically anytime we are in a potentially life-or-death situation, we need to be able to respond quickly and with intense energy, if need be. Some of the more obviously potential life-threatening events include car crashes, being trapped in a burning building, getting caught in a massive earthquake or other natural disaster, being held up at gunpoint, having a heart attack, bleeding excessively, or choking. Or, even witnessing someone else in any of these situations while they're occurring, may require you to respond in emergency mode.

Sometimes danger is completely unpredictable—an electrical fire could erupt inside your house while you're sleeping, your dog could chew up his leash and bolt out into oncoming traffic, or one of your car's tires could blow out on the freeway at sixty-five miles per hour. Sometimes the risk of danger is present, but the level is very low. In these situations one might decide that the chances of something really seriously bad happening aren't worth avoiding the potential for benefit or fun, for example flying in a commercial jet, downhill skiing on an intermediate level run, or riding in an elevator in a hundred-story high rise in order to be able to see the most spectacular view of a city. Sometimes the risk of danger is highly likely and probably not worth whatever may be considered a potential benefit, for instance trying to emulate a stunt you just saw in a superhero movie like leaping from the rooftop of a twenty-story building onto another building ten feet away, knowing that you haven't even attempted a long jump since you were in junior high school and even back then you weren't very good at it.

Drama queens, however, don't tend to evaluate the risks accurately and they tend to react habitually as though anything with even a remote possibility of going badly is the same as an actual crisis occurring in the moment. Hence, they fail to make conscious choices or decisions about which risks to take and which ones to avoid. Plus, many drama queens seem to actually invite danger or drama wherever they go even though they'll have others believe that the danger simply finds them. They may even become indignant and offended if you suggest that they have something to do with creating the drama.

Drama queens often unknowingly manufacture danger in their minds because they perceive a situation through hypersensitive lenses, seeing nuances that others may not notice at all. In other words, even while things are going smoothly, they'll remain vigilant, watching out for the mere chance that something might go wrong. If you believe in self-fulfilling prophecies, then you almost have to wonder whether drama queens may inadvertently be setting up disasters because they're so convinced danger is right around the corner anyway.

The reality of life is that many random situations will appear to be emergencies, requiring rapid assessment to most everyone. But upon closer examination, these scenarios don't actually require emergency mode reactivity. And while non-drama queens are able to turn off their adrenaline switch before it gets out of control and takes over their actions, drama queens can't. Non-drama queens would say, "Oops! False alarm—thought that car was about to smash into the lamppost but the driver just cut his turn too sharply." The drama queen, however, seems compelled to go all the way through an emergency response, even if she discovers along the way that nothing really bad has happened or is going to happen.

For example, here's an ambiguous scenario that doesn't turn out to be a true red-alert alarm, but could clearly be difficult to distinguish and, therefore, might be very upsetting to a drama queen. Imagine you witness a child falling from a tree branch five feet above the ground. She lands on her hands and knees and screams for help, with tears pouring down her red, puffy cheeks like water gushing from a broken fire hydrant. At this moment you think she might be in a lot of pain and may possibly have broken or sprained her leg or wrist. But you also know that she is conscious and alert. Of course, if you then see that she is bleeding, there's a possibility that she may pass out or lose too much blood and would, in fact, require emergency medical care. On the other hand, she may not be physically hurt at all, and her tears and pleas for help may simply be a product of her being scared and in need of emotional nurturance. Clearly, in either case, it wouldn't make any sense to take your sweet time strolling up to this child. Rather, you would need to kick into gear immediately to find out how badly the child is hurt. But it also wouldn't make sense to dial 911 in a panicked state such that the child's suffering becomes secondary to your own reactivity. Not to mention, you wouldn't even be able to adequately explain to the emergency operator what the problem is.

At this point, there are no indicators that this child is any more hurt than just mildly banged up. I'm certainly not suggesting that it would be wrong to call in emergency forces, but it really may not be necessary. Nor am I advocating that untrained people become sidewalk nurses or doctors. A layperson isn't going to be able to diagnose the severity of a physical injury. But we generally have certain indicators that tell us whether something is a real physical crisis requiring immediate medical care or whether a small delay and more thorough assessment might minimize the trauma and drama.

Such a situation would generally activate anyone's adrenaline pump, especially since this scenario involves a helpless child who is definitely in *need* of some sort of attention and care. But as a drama queen, you might have difficulty calming down and moving forward once the child's tears are dried, the bandages are applied, and she's making her way over to the sandbox to check out her new set of buckets and shovels. Even if you refrain from hauling the child off to emergency care despite her demonstration of being fine, you can't stop from imagining everything that "might" have happened. And you go home and tell the story over and over again to whoever will listen. Even though this scenario turned out not to be such a big deal, you can't let it go.

There are many other types of scenarios we might encounter outside the realm of physical life-death situations that would cause an intense reaction in the immediate moment. But again, even though the scenario is intense and bound to stir up feelings, it doesn't necessarily warrant a drama queen response. For instance let's look at Kevin—a twenty-eight-year-old sales manager who lived in a constant state of stress and agitation. While he never intended to make other people miserable, his perpetual state of distress and reactivity inevitably took others down a stress path with him.

Kevin's boss, Eileen, made demands above and beyond normal levels of Kevin's time and energy appropriate from her employee, and she tended to turn everything into a crisis. And Kevin, being prone to his own over-reactivity, felt like he was on a firefighter's drill schedule all of the time. Though he liked his job when he was out in the field and away from Eileen, he would have to be in her presence and under her watch a good portion of each day. And by the time he'd be free to call it quits for the day, he would be an emotional mess. Sometimes he felt like he would never be able to have a moment of peace or relaxation. And because he was running on empty most of the time and didn't know how to unwind, he never really recharged his battery before he'd have return to work, leaving him that much more vulnerable to Eileen's tyrannical style.

Almost daily, or at least weekly, Eileen would threaten Kevin's job, telling him that the company was on the brink of going belly-up at any moment. Of course, this went on for years and the company neither folded nor did Kevin lose his job. In fact, the company continued to make a profit each year and he continued to receive nice year-end bonuses. Though Kevin also rated relatively high on the drama queen scale even before he ever met the likes of Eileen, he was the lovable drama queen type and truly didn't want to make big deals out small things. Eileen, on the other hand, resembled the vampire-like queen and she could care less about the impact of her behavior or expectations on others. But while Kevin didn't like how he kept buying into Eileen's insanity and allowing her reality to take over his whole existence, he didn't know how to stop reacting to Eileen's tirades and hysterics.

Poor Kevin would go home each night and complain to his wife, Leslie, about how awful his job was and he would get her to fear that they were in a crisis as well. Eileen's spiraling energy invaded Kevin's entire existence. He couldn't relax, and he was starting to drive his wife nuts too. Leslie tried to soothe and calm her husband, reminding him that Eileen was all bark and no bite. But he simply couldn't shake off her influence because he wasn't really seeing that he had any choices about his reactivity and resulting responses: that is, he didn't realize that he could either ignore her threats or find another job.

It turns out Kevin's buttons were getting pushed even more than usual because Eileen had a very similar temperament to Kevin's father. Like Kevin's father, Eileen felt greatly entitled to get everything she demanded from others, no matter how unreasonable her demands might have been. Though Kevin was a highly accomplished and intelligent man, anytime he would be around someone like Eileen (and especially around her, since she was an authority figure), he felt as helpless to take care of himself as he had felt in the presence of his dad. He had trouble recognizing that he had the power to choose how to react to Eileen even if she never changed a thing about herself. But instead of setting healthy boundaries with her and not allowing her to get under his skin, he would work overtime to try to appease her and would inevitably get burnt out.

No doubt, many people would have a hard time working for someone like Eileen. She was a really tough cookie who could easily make anyone vulnerable to a drama queen syndrome. But even though Kevin didn't initially realize his own role in creating his drama, at some point he started to recognize that she wasn't going to change and if he wanted to enjoy life and minimize his stress, he needed to learn how to modify his reactions to her or get out. Of course, it was highly possible that Kevin might have lost his job had he stopped jumping through all the hoops she set out for him. But regardless, he still wasn't in a life or death situation and his adrenalin pump was working overtime unnecessarily. In reality, he did not have to take any of her crap anymore.

Kevin eventually learned that he didn't actually have to comply with the demands of others and he didn't have to react like a puppet on a string being mishandled. His wife was certainly grateful for him to learn that important life lesson. He ultimately did give Eileen his resignation and ended up starting a company of his own.

Kevin, like many other drama queens, had to learn how not to allow other people's negative behavior to run and ruin his life. And even though he rid himself of Eileen on a permanent basis, there's no way to escape all negativity. Thankfully, he eventually realized that he better get some new tools. Basically, Kevin had to learn how to react appropriately without overreacting. As Kevin learned, it's also in your best interest to embrace the notion that just because other people behave badly doesn't mean you have to follow suit. And more often than not, the catastrophes you fear often never even happen at all.

The Solutions

The R.E.A.C.T Tool

Though there's no magical formula for becoming able to let go of unnecessary stress and go with the flow, you might benefit significantly from using the R.E.A.C.T. assessment tool, an acronym for Reality, Emergency, Action, Consequence, and Thought. This tool can be used in any scenario as long you're not in an imminent life or death situation. For instance, if you see a car headed right for your driver's side door at fifty miles per hour, don't stop to think about what you need to do. Get the heck out of the way with as minimal damage to yourself and others as possible. But short of anything this immediate, you can use this tool wherever you are. At some point, it may even become like an alternative reflex: something you just do, and don't even have to give it much thought. And by then, it will happen so fast, you might not even realize that you've gone through a conscious assessment process. Here's how each part of the process works.

Reality

Most situations in life truly aren't a big deal or at least they won't be as soon as they're adequately resolved. And while some scenarios may seem like a big deal initially, with a delay in response you will discover that you don't really need to take any action at all, because it's merely a small hiccup that won't matter in the grand scheme of things. But for those situations where a reaction is required, we must first assess the reality. Thus, this reality assessment phase is aimed at getting a handle on what is actually going on in the moment, not what you believe or fear will happen sometime later on, even if only a moment later.

The first step is to verbalize aloud or in your head what it is that you are observing. This is a highly important component because it provides the necessary piece to interrupt the knee-jerk reflex so well developed in drama queens. Please understand that I know this may sound impossible to implement. But while it may initially be hard, since the drama queen within you will want to dominate your actions and hold you hostage, you can do this. And I promise once you've put this tool into effect several times, you'll find it easier and easier to soothe and subdue the queen. It's worth a try anyway. After all, aren't you a little tired of bowing and responding dutifully to a force that isn't always steering you in the best direction?

Next, in order to accurately assess the reality of a situation it's best to ask yourself the following questions. Of course, these can be modified according to your personal preferences or the specifics of the situation.

1. Does what I'm observing or experiencing constitute a life-or-death situation that a) *relates to myself* and b) is occurring *at this very moment*?

2. Is what I'm observing or experiencing happening a) to someone else and b) at this very moment?

3. Is what I'm observing or experiencing something I'm *projecting* is going to happen in the near future but is not actually happening at this very moment?

Now let's look at these one at a time.

#1. Does what I'm observing or experiencing constitute a life-or-death situation that a) *relates to myself* and b) is occurring *at this very moment*? (Clearly, if the answer is yes, then your f-f-f response will kick in automatically and you will do whatever you need to do to survive).

Though you'll be well equipped to respond with your body's inherent capacity to fight, flee, or freeze when in danger, there are a few things you need to consider when you're not in any crisis state. Remember, I'm not going to mess with your inherent f-f-f response, but it's very important that you understand this question fully and why I'm suggesting you try asking it over and over again. In my experience if you start routinely asking this question when you feel the over-reactivity response germinating in your body, you'll become very sensitive to the answer dictated by actual realty. And, at some point you won't need to ask this question because you'll simply be responding with emergency gear when reality calls for it and, for those non-emergency moments that at one point would have elicited an over-the-top response, you'll have new, built-in reactions. But for now until this becomes as natural to you as reaching out to scratch an itch, I encourage you to pay attention to this assessment question more closely.

Also, let's look at the clause "relates to myself" because this distinction from "relating to someone else" (loved one, random stranger, animal, and so forth) may very well make a big difference in how you respond to an emergency situation. For instance, if my pant leg catches on fire, I'm going to roll on the ground as quickly as possible to suffocate the oxygen fueling the flames. Or, if I can get to an ample source of water quickly enough, I'm going to submerge my leg in water. Otherwise, if I do nothing I would likely fry my skin or have my whole body burn up. And, as much as the latter scenario might get me more attention than just telling someone about a fire on my pant leg, I'm not going to let that happen because I'm going to be inclined to fight for my own survival and prevent myself from experiencing excruciating pain. And, in case you don't believe me that you would try to save yourself in this kind of situation, then you may be suffering from severe clinical depression, and I *strongly* encourage you to please seek immediate professional help. But assuming that we are on the same page about what you would do in this situation, then we both agree that you're in a situation that implies imminent harm to yourself and it's you who must do something about it to ensure your safety and survival.

But what if I see someone across the street with his pant leg on fire and there are cars racing by? Clearly, it wouldn't be the wisest reaction for me to bolt across the street, putting myself at risk for being hit by a moving vehicle and potentially jeopardizing my own life. But if the guy looked to be in shock and wasn't making any motions toward preventing himself from getting engulfed by the flames, I may shout at the top of my lungs,

"Hey buddy, get on the ground and start rolling," hoping that this directive would be helpful in setting his survival skills in motion. And if no one else were around to help him (even if just to give him some comfort for his scary moment, once he eliminates the flame), I would probably cross the street and head over to him, but I would wait until the traffic cleared.

My ability to react in service of helping someone else in imminent danger would be even more subdued if I were to turn on the local news, capturing this same man on camera. And my reactivity would decrease even more if I were to hear about this scenario after the fact. As you can see, our ability to respond effectively to emergencies has everything to do with how much control we have over a situation, who's involved, and the immediacy of a situation. And for the most part, we have the greatest control over ourselves (not over other people) and only in the immediate moment.

Hence, the "at this very moment" clause is also highly significant because it helps determine the level of reactivity warranted. Remember a major disadvantage about being stuck in drama queen mode is the tendency to *project* danger or catastrophe. And while the projected danger seems like a real thing that will occur, more often than not, the situation imagined will never actually occur. And even if a feared situation arises in reality, it will often turn out far more positively or certainly not as bad as had been imagined. (Of course, sometimes drama queens project a phenomenally positive outcome that doesn't usually occur and then they are faced with intense disappointment.) The point is that far too much time and energy gets wasted on the "what ifs" instead dealing with "what is." So the answer to this question needs to rely on what is happening *now*, not what might happen in the future.

If the answer to question number 1 is "yes," then an emergency response definitely is warranted. (And drama queens are usually very good at these!) However, just be sure not to stay in emergency mode once the crisis is resolved. Of course, if you've been traumatized by a real emergency, such as a rape or other violent assault, you may not be able to let what's happened to you become a memory as opposed to something you continually relive. If this is the case, you may be suffering from P.T.S.D. and will probably need professional help. (Refer to the last chapter for more on this.)

#2. Is what I'm observing or experiencing happening a) to someone else and b) at this very moment?

Clearly, many people become over-reactors because they are highly sensitive. The world impinges on them more than on others. Hence, they may feel things more deeply than do others. So naturally if something bad is happening to anyone and a drama queen sees someone suffering firsthand or even secondhand by another's report, he or she's likely to have strong internal reactions to such events.

Now, there's nothing wrong with compassion and empathy. In fact, if only everyone would get an extra dose of these loving attributes, we'd live in a much better world. Sadly, however, while we might feel compassion for other people's hardships, we can't always make it our mission to rescue everyone from adversity. It's just not possible. So in order to thrive within our own lives, sometimes we have to refrain from trying to save or rescue someone who appears to be in harm's way, even if this goes against the grain of who we are, and especially if our heroic gestures are driven by a need to get accolades or elevated status. The reverence simply isn't worth the potential danger to ourselves. Thus, we must pick and choose our battles carefully.

This is by no means a mandate—just something to think about if this is a common way that your drama queen syndrome manifests. And if you're a significant other reading this, be careful that you aren't subtly or overtly giving the drama queen you love a message that his/her worth is dependent on how much she/he gives care to others, especially if that comes at the price of not taking good care of herself/himself. Otherwise, you will actually be feeding the drama queen syndrome and potentially making it worse, not better.

Hiking the Real Mountains, Sliding over the Molehills

Basically, I recommend that if you're in a situation where someone other than yourself is in imminent danger, and you can be helpful without harming yourself, then feel free to react (even if in a very big way). But if you're putting yourself in danger, please start to think twice.

#3. Is what I'm observing or experiencing something I'm *projecting* is going to happen in the near future but is not actually happening at this very moment?

Projection can be a great asset, but sometimes the process of trying to foreshadow the future can be a disaster and potentially make our lives miserable. So if you tend to get into the projection game or the endless cycle of "what ifs," then it's definitely time to take a few deep breaths and calm down. Then move on through the rest of this tool, skipping E for Emergency, since a projected emergency is not the same as a real emergency.

If you're having trouble determining whether or not you're truly in danger or whether you're projecting, ask yourself if other people would agree that what you're observing or experiencing constitutes an emergency. If no one else around you is responding intensely, then there's a good chance your drama queen buttons have been pushed and you need to interrupt your tendency to overreact. For instance, if you're on an airplane in flight and you encounter heavy turbulence, take a quick look around you at the flight attendants. If they're still bouncing around out of their seats serving beverages or gathering trash, with smiles on their faces, there's a pretty good chance you have nothing to fear. Their behavior probably indicates the turbulence is not unusual for that particular flight. Even if they are required to buckle up themselves, it's highly unlikely the plane is going down.

So from here forward, make a commitment to assess the reality of a situation, even if only for a split second. And by taking an extra moment to delay your reaction, you can then *choose* how to respond. And more often than not, you'll become more levelheaded and possibly even better at responding to true crisis situations. (But let's hope you don't have to deal with many of those!)

The Solutions

Emergency

If what you observe during your reality check is a true emergency, then your body will command you to fight, flee, or freeze. As I've already said, thankfully we're hardwired with these responses right at our fingertips so we don't have to do too much thinking. But if you're still having a hard time believing that you'll keep your f-f-f capacity intact, especially if you're convinced that your survival mechanism has been permanently screwed up, then it might help if you reframe your thinking. Basically, while other people tend to live in an at-rest state and their bodies kick into alarm mode when necessary, drama queens live in survival mode because they don't trust that their bodies will do the right thing. But since many emergencies aren't life or death situations, it's still a good idea to be conscious of your course of action.

It's time you stop micromanaging yourself and the rest of the world, and instead focus your energy on building trust in your inherent capacities. I can guess what you're thinking—"This doc is nuts." But remember, I've been in you shoes. I was once a high level over-reactor (getting calmer every day) and I've never lost my ability to see danger when it's present. Think of it this way. Do you focus on making yourself breathe on a regular basis (not while you're practicing deep relaxation or yoga)? I would guess not. Why? Because you trust your body will take care of this. So all I'm asking is that you allow your body to do what it's already programmed to do. And unless you're living in a war zone, purposefully putting yourself in dangerous conditions hoping to be harmed or even killed, or your job has built in danger (such as, firefighter, police officer, private detective, and other such professions), you're probably not going to encounter too many emergencies on a day-to-day basis. And by the way, if you are someone who is suicidal, please seek professional help immediately.

You might also be skeptical because at some point in your life you reacted by instinct and it didn't serve you well. In other words, you have hard-core evidence from past experience that your body froze when you think you should have fought, or you fled when you think you should have fought, or some other combination. The way I look at that, however, is how do you know you should have done something else? You're alive, right? So your body still served you well and maybe it's your ego or some other factor that's messin' with your mind.

Action

Once you've assessed reality and determined that there is no crisis requiring emergency response, you now have to *decide* what actions to take. Once again, I emphasize *decide* because the whole point of this exercise is to increase your ability to refrain from automatic reflexive over-reactivity.

Here's an example. You promised your sweetie you'd be home for dinner by six p.m. and you encounter unexpected traffic. You know that she had a very special meal planned to celebrate your new job. As a drama queen, your first reaction is to start to panic and you worry intensely about the disappointment she'll feel when you call and tell her you won't make it on time. In your mind, you're already jumping ahead to divorce court and working yourself up with each passing moment.

After a few minutes of this, you reach for your cell phone and you discover your battery is dead. A double whammy: traffic and dead cell. Without new tools, you're likely to have this experience ruin your whole night. But by using the R.E.A.C.T tool instead, you would assess reality and quickly recognize this isn't a crisis (unless you make it one) and, therefore, doesn't require emergency response. Rather it requires making a thoughtful decision about the best course of action. A couple of options come to my mind. But as with any scenario, the options should be weighed in your mind according to your particular life circumstances.

For instance, you could get off the freeway, find a pay phone, and call your sweetie, apologizing for the situation and indicating that you, too, are disappointed that you're not being able to make it home in time as promised. You could offer to do something to make it up to her in the near future. And/or you could find out whether she would consider keeping the meal warm until you're able to get there. Of course, if you choose this option, you need to be sincere, but not dramatic. And whatever you do, don't embellish your story to make it sound like you're a victim. As much as you may feel like a victim, you wouldn't qualify as one. Rather, you'd just be one of the many commuters whose arrival time became lengthened because two accidents left a few lanes blocked and backed up the normal flow of traffic.

Now if you're someone who repeatedly runs late, then you might need to be a bit more accountable and take responsibility for not having left work early enough to avoid this situation. But, again, I wouldn't want to make a big deal of it. You're human and you can't foresee traffic patterns. Hey, even meteorologists who get paid tons of money to forecast the weather routinely screw up. So cut yourself some slack. Shit happens.

Consequences

The actions we take will have a big impact on the reactions of others. Sometimes the consequences will be fairly predictable because you've already had multiple experiences where the actions you took led to a particular consequence. For instance, if your daughter is sensitive to criticism and becomes defensive anytime you comment disapprovingly on her behavior, then you can pretty much guess that the next time you criticize her that she's going to become defensive. (By the way, that doesn't mean you shouldn't make your comments, but don't be surprised by the reaction.)

Sometimes the outcome of an event is completely unimaginable, leaving you taken by surprise. But regardless of predictability, one thing that's for certain is that every action has a reaction. Hence, it's important to choose your responses knowing that there will be consequences: sometimes positive or neutral, sometimes negative, even though you might not be able to know for certain what that consequence will be.

Now for non-drama queens, this is not a big deal. They think through potential consequences, but they don't worry so much about them. In contrast, drama queens tend to project catastrophic consequences regardless of the actions they take—as though their actions don't really matter or that they have no real control over anything. And while it's true that we can't control how the world or the people in it will respond to our actions, there are usually some pretty strong correlations between our actions and the reactions of others. For instance, if we are calm and collected around others and don't get too worked up about the little stuff, we will usually have a calming effect on those around us. On the flip side, if we are nervous, chronically upset, agitated, or fully engaged in our best drama queen performance, we will usually tend to illicit more negative responses from others like irritation, aggravation, and/or avoidance. And this, of course, reinforces our sensitivity buttons addressed in the previous chapter. But, by assessing the consequences of our actions we can start to really understand cause and effect or at least become familiar with the likely pairings of action and outcome.

Peter, a third-year law-school student, was having great difficulty managing his time and juggling the responsibilities of his course load, homework, and part-time job. He had grown up in a family environment where he was the golden child and he could do no wrong in anyone's eyes. And, for the most part, he had very few responsibilities other than attending school and getting good grades. His parents were happy to support him through his higher education and they were very proud of him.

Though this might seem like a cushy life for someone who may have endured hardship or childhood mistreatment, Peter was not as fortunate as one might imagine. In fact, he actually became quite disadvantaged over many others in the world because he had developed very little capacity to deal with daily problems or hardship of any kind. And because he had a very demonstrative personality he couldn't help but let others know when things didn't go just the way he had planned or imagined them to be. Many of his peers envied him because he seemed so privileged. "What the hell does he have to complain about? That guy gets everything handed to him on a silver platter," many would think. Basically, even though Peter was a pretty decent guy with good values, many people perceived him as an arrogant, entitled a-hole.

The reality was that Peter never really had to experience negative consequences for his actions while growing up. If he got a bad grade in a class, his parents would talk the teacher into changing it—coming up with some elaborate story as to why he wasn't able to perform up to his usual standards. He was never required to clean his room or do any chores because the live-in nanny took care of everything for him. He had never even started a washing machine or washed a dish until he moved out of his parents' home and started attending law school. Then, he was faced with managing his time, keeping track of his responsibilities, and taking care of his basic needs without anyone bailing him out when things got too stressful for him.

Peter's childhood circumstances left him with a faulty belief that he wouldn't have to be responsible or accountable for his behavior or choices. And he learned that if he threw a tantrum, he'd get whatever he wanted. What a shock to his system when he got a C in one of his classes because he failed a final exam (due to late night partying and not studying) and couldn't get his professor to change his grade. He was certain that he could manipulate the professor to cut him some slack. But no such luck, and he found himself at an important crossroad in his life. Peter had a lightbulb moment when he realized that if he wanted to succeed in his career and in relationships with others, he needed to take responsibility for his actions and accept the consequences. This also eventually helped him become better able to deal with life's daily stressors and not get so wigged out over trivial matters. Let me tell you, this wasn't easy—he fought this reality every step of the way. But eventually he became humbled and learned how to consider other people's feelings and needs as well as keeping track of his own.

So hopefully you're already ahead of Peter, knowing that your actions have consequences. But I recommend that you continue to fine tune your awareness in this area. In doing so, you will continue to lay the foundation for changing your drama queen behavior into something more tranquil and serene. Then, you will begin to see different results and not the ones you fear.

Thought

This may seem silly to have "thought" at the end of all of this, since all four others steps also involve thinking. But this step is meant to be a preventative step to future drama queeny responses. So in this phase of the tool, I'm suggesting that you look back and review the chain of events from the original stimulus to the actions you took and the consequences that followed.

So take a moment or two and reflect on the last time you found yourself in a triggering situation where your drama queen behavior erupted and evaluate it all the way through the R.E.A.C.T. method. This kind of thinking will help you become more and more conscious of your over-reactivity and how to interrupt it somewhere in the process.

And please keep in mind that your progress in diminishing your drama queen behaviors isn't measured by perfection. It's not likely that you will read this once and then never again respond with over-reactivity. The measure of success is in seeing some progress along the way. Maybe tomorrow your car will break down because you hadn't remembered to take it in for the recommended 30,000 mile service or you didn't think that regular service actually mattered to a car's performance. And you react with severe anxiety, fear of catastrophe, and all the other drama queen gestures. But twenty minutes into your freak-out state you're able to say something like, "Hey, this too shall pass, and I'll get through this—

this isn't a life or death situation. I'm responsible for creating this mess, but it's fixable. Inconvenient—yes. But disaster—no."

If you were able to have this thought, then you would have made great progress in taming your drama queen response. So while this tool may seem tedious to implement while you're initially trying it out, be patient. Give it a whirl a few times and see whether it can help soothe you and help prevent or lessen the reactions and behaviors that tend to leave you feeling depleted and embarrassed. And you don't even have to tell anyone that you're trying out a new way of being. You can just do it—and watch and see whether other people's responses toward you improve as well.

Chapter 6

Changing Your Expectations

Expectations are a natural part of being human. Hey, this may even be true within the animal kingdom, especially among mammals. But I must confess I'm not up-to-date on the latest animal brain research. And since we know that it's unlikely for any pooches, kitties, or other critters to be reading this, I'll just stick with the explanation of what I know about human expectations: that is, how certain types of expectations can result in exacerbating the drama queen syndrome, and possibly even play a role in creating it.

Since expectations are inherently part of the human experience, then there's clearly nothing wrong with having them. But the critical clause is "as long as they are reasonable and based on actual agreements." For instance, as far as relationship experts are concerned, it's considered healthy to expect an intimate partner to contribute equally to the overall functioning of the unit. So if you hold this belief and you have checked out with your partner that he too believes in this underlying premise for a healthy relationship, then you have reasonable grounds to expect that each of you will perform certain functions in the relationship. For instance, if you make a verbal agreement with your significant other that he will be responsible for taking out the trash and you for paying the bills, it's reasonable to expect that your sweetie will be bringing out those smelly containers curbside on trash collection day. And, it's also reasonable for him to assume that you're going to fire off those payments when they become due. Conversely, this expectation would not be reasonable if either or both of the following conditions existed: (1) you and your sweetie don't share the same belief about the partnership aspect of the relationship and/or (2) you never actually had a discussion about what roles or functions each of you were going to fulfill. In other words, it's not reasonable to expect your mate to take out the trash if you only made this agreement in your own head and never actually got his consent.

Not only do we have expectations about how we and other people should behave, we also have expectations of how events should transpire. For instance, if you're invited to a black-tie affair and you've been to a few of these events in the past, you'll probably anticipate that the event will include a sit-down dinner with fancy plates and possibly even cutlery made of actual silver. Of course, that wouldn't necessarily be how everyone would set up that kind of event, but it would be reasonable to assume fanciness over casualness, based on your previous experience and the common definition of a black-tie affair. Or, if you live in a large metropolitan city and you've been told that a restaurant you're interested in dining at is on the pricey side, you can reasonably expect that you won't find a meal for less than twenty to thirty bucks. Of course, if the person who conveyed this information is someone who's never been to any eating establishment other than fast-food joints and/or she comes from an impoverished background, then you might not share a similar scale in terms of what a pricey meal would be. She might be appalled at any meal over ten dollars. Conversely, someone who's used to dining where the rich and famous hang out might not even bat an eye at dropping a couple hundred bucks for a meal.

Though we all have expectations, more often than not, many of us have considerable trouble keeping our expectations reasonable, and this seems to be even more pronounced for those who are members of the drama queen society. Because so many of us drama queens came from dysfunctional backgrounds and our society is committed to countless ideas and beliefs that foster unhealthy expectations, we often end up expecting things of the world and other people that simply can't be fulfilled, or certainly not with any consistency or regularity. Some of these expectations may be fairly inconsequential, such as expecting a spouse to know your muscles ache and to give you a massage without you having even told her that you're in pain, or expecting a bank teller to open up another window for your transaction because you're in a hurry and you don't have time to wait in line. Other expectations can be very consequential, such as allowing yourself to amass $20,000 of debt, not being able to make payments on it, and then expecting your best friend to bail you out. While the disappointment of unrealized unreasonable expectations can be upsetting to anyone, for drama queens these disappointments tend to be far more problematic and possibly even devastating. Let me explain further.

I've already alluded to the idea that our expectations about how the world—and the people in it—should operate, directly correlates with the drama queen syndrome. Hence, if we have reasonable expectations of ourselves, other living beings, and the world at large, we're less likely to experience disappointment, annoyance, and aggravation (several of the emotional states that trigger drama queen behavior). And, we're more likely to have smoother sailing in our day-to-day existence. In turn, by having stable energy we can put our focus on enjoying life and achieving our goals for contentment, improved relationships, and greater productivity.

Conversely, if we have unreasonable expectations, we can easily get into trouble by setting ourselves up for intense negative emotions and over-reactivity—the classic experiences of a drama queen. Plus, we may even have a hard time taking responsibility for ourselves because we might continually expect others to take care of our needs when we should be pulling our own weight. Or, sometimes an imbalance occurs because we take *too* much responsibility for other people and/or for things we have no control over, leaving us dry and used up. In turn, we may knowingly or unknowingly expect others to do the same for us.

Naturally this system is most likely going to fail unless we have full consent from others, stating that they agree to operate by these assumptions. But even if we could actually get such consent from each and every person we encounter, no one can meet our needs perfectly, let alone accurately predict what these needs might be at any given moment. Thus, by operating within this dysfunctional system (a form of codependency), we will often perceive that we've been cheated out of something we deserve, and then have a negative emotional reaction. Plus, even if people could be trained to cooperate with this arrangement, how in the world would we ever be able to get the cosmos to play by these rules? Did you ever encounter an earthquake or tornado that stopped on your command?

If what I'm saying resonates with you, please understand that I'm not trying to shame or make fun of you. Rather, I just want you, drama queen, to begin seeing that keeping alive unrealistic expectations renders you stuck in a vicious cycle that will not serve your purpose of gaining tranquility.

So how does a drama queen develop reasonable expectations and hence foster more mellowness? I've found there to be three very important interrelated steps: (1) by understanding the differences between realistic and unrealistic expectations, (2) by adopting a thriver mentality, and (3) by developing healthy core beliefs about how the world and the things in it should operate.

Changing Your Expectations

Understanding the Differences between Realistic and Unrealistic Expectations

The ability to fine tune your expectation meter and keep it operating in the reasonable zone can be very tricky. After all, oftentimes we have expectations on a less than conscious level, so we're not even aware of them. At other times, we may know we have expectations, but we're afraid to admit them openly and honestly because we think we're not supposed to have any. However, as normal as it is to have expectations, we need to become conscious of what they are at any given moment and knock them down to an appropriate level when they get too inflated. We also need to be aware of when we don't expect enough from a situation so that we don't allow others to treat us like doormats and then become prone to displacing our expectations inappropriately. For example, imagine that you get invited out to dinner, and the way the invitation is presented would lead most people to assume that the inviter is going to pick up the tab. But, if you have very low self-esteem and don't believe you deserve a free meal, you might insist on paying for your share when the check arrives. But, if you, in turn, become annoyed that the person allowed you to pay (consciously or unconsciously), then the next time you go out with your friends where everyone usually pays for their own stuff, you very well might expect they'll pick up the tab because you got "cheated" in the other situation. You can see that this is a recipe for disaster.

Henry, a mid-thirties performing artist, never felt he was good enough at his craft and he would always act surprised by the validating applause he usually received. But deep down inside, he actually expected his audiences to demonstrate appreciation for all of his performances, regardless of the quality of his delivery. Hence, if he got anything less than a standing ovation, he would become emotionally wounded and overreact with dismal negativity, self-criticisms, and disdain for the audience's lack of appreciation for his efforts. Though he didn't realize it, he was basically screwing himself, because he couldn't outwardly admit that he had

121

any expectations to begin with. And since he couldn't even acknowledge having any expectations at all, he certainly couldn't identify those that were unreasonable. But, once he finally understood that having expectations wasn't the problem, but rather, that having *unreasonable* expectations was, then he could begin to make headway on becoming more realistic about how much other people could actually be expected to fill up his self-esteem holes.

"So how do I distinguish reasonable from unreasonable expectations?" you might be asking. Well, I think it helps to think of expectations on a continuum with "very unrealistic" on one end to "perfectly appropriate" on the other end. Also, when trying to determine what's reasonable, it's also important to take into account the specifics of the situation and/or the person you're expecting something from. While not always true, for the most part you can probably expect more from an intimate relationship partner than from a casual acquaintance and certainly more than from a stranger. And, you can probably safely generalize your expectations from one situation to another if they have multiple overlapping features. For instance, if you frequently go to the theater to see movies, it would be reasonable to expect that any theater you attend is most likely going to have a concession stand, start the movie and/or previews at the times listed online or in the newspaper, and have a seat available for you as long as you arrive early enough to purchase a ticket. But it wouldn't be reasonable to assume that a particular aisle seat in a particular row is going to be available if you choose to arrive five minutes before show time on a Saturday night for a new blockbuster release.

Since your life will have unique nuances that I cannot possibly predict, then clearly I'm not able to give you an exhaustive list of all reasonable expectations for each and every scenario or person you encounter. But hopefully the descriptions below will serve as guidelines for you to use when assessing the reasonableness of your expectations.

Concerning expectations of other people, it's reasonable to suppose that people will fulfill all agreements that have been articulated and understood by both parties. And if someone finds or decides that he/she cannot fulfill an agreement made with you, then it's reasonable to expect this to be communicated. It's also reasonable to expect that the people in your inner circle (friends, family, significant others) will treat you with respect and care.

Mind you, just because it's reasonable to expect these things from others doesn't mean that they will actually come through on their promises. People make mistakes, they get angry, and sometimes they even retaliate. Or sometimes people don't take the agreements they make seriously in the first place. Even very well-intentioned, ethical people break agreements at times, though usually not intentionally. Some people breach contracts without any awareness or memory of the agreement in the first place. And yet others only say "yes" under pressure because they don't think they have the right to say "no" to a request. The fact is that humans screw up from time to time, and this is just the nature of the beast!

Also, while it's reasonable to assume that people you're closest to will have your back, if any of them demonstrate a pattern of not caring about promises they make or of mistreating you, then it's no longer reasonable to expect that you will get what you desire from these individuals, regardless of any agreements made. Plus, if you are of sound mind, it's never reasonable to expect someone to read your mind; that is, to know what your needs or preferences are without you articulating them. Even people who consider themselves to be soul mates cannot accurately read their partner's mind. Granted, if you have repeatedly told someone whom you love that you like something a certain way each and every time and you've never changed your mind, then it would be reasonable to expect this someone to remember this about you and for you not to have to restate the agreement over and over again. For instance, if your lover agrees to have dinner with you every Sunday night, then you should be able to count on sharing this time together each week, unless some unforeseeable event arises or something else takes precedence and the change is communicated to you.

Plus, regardless of how reasonable your expectation may be, if you're committed to a flaky person, it is *you* who should change your expectations if you want to stay in the relationship and not keep going to an empty well for water. Or, you might want to consider getting out. Because, no matter how much we may like to control other people's actions, we simply can't *make* other people change or force them to do what we expect of them (unless you render someone in a victim position, and you don't want to do that).

Concerning expectations of events or situations, it's reasonable to expect that legally-run, reputable entities will deliver services, events, or products as promised, or as close to what's promised as possible. For instance, if you're buying an Accord from a Honda dealership, it's safe to assume you will be getting an actual Accord, not an Altima (from Nissan) disguised as an Accord. But even in clean-cut situations, there's still room for error. Stuff happens and things won't always turn out the way they're planned. For instance, let's say you plan an outdoor wedding in a month that typically has very little rainfall. But what if the rain gods have another plan in mind? As you can see, even when you think something should happen in a certain way, there are many things that can shake up the pot!

If you are trying something new and have little information or experience with it, then it's usually a good idea to have very few expectations. You could just be spontaneous and take what comes or you could try to find out as much information as possible to gauge your expectations. But even if you get information in advance, many descriptions of things are very subjective. Hence, how something is described may very well be fitting to the person doing the describing, yet not at all fitting to you. For instance, if you meet a new person who invites you to a party and she tells you it will be "tons of fun" but you really don't know how much you have in common with this person, then it's probably better to go with a wait-and-see attitude rather than get your hopes up too high. Her idea of fun might be pulling weeds out of her garden in 105 degree temperatures whereas your idea of fun is drinking a Margarita and playing group video games in someone's air-conditioned living room.

To illustrate further how to distinguish reasonable from unreasonable expectations, here are some specific scenarios. But again, keep it in mind that I can't give an example of every single situation you may encounter in your life where you would likely have some expectations. So just use these scenarios as a springboard for looking at the situations that have arisen in your own life where expectations come into play.

- If you purchase an article of clothing from a well-known department store and the label says 100 percent cotton, then it's reasonable to assume that the material is, in fact, pure cotton. Conversely, if you buy the same article of clothing off the back of someone's pick-up truck, you might get lucky and have the fabric actually be what it says, but it's a gamble and you shouldn't be too bummed if you discover it's actually polyester.

- If you read a description of a new restaurant and several reviews from critics you tend to agree with, then it's reasonable to assume that you'll probably enjoy your meal when you patronize the establishment. But there's no guarantee because food tastes are very subjective. Conversely, if you try a restaurant you've never heard of before and you know nothing about it, it wouldn't be reasonable to expect anything specific other than the fact that the place will serve you food. If it has an A or B rating on the outside window, then you could also expect to avoid contracting food poisoning. But, there would be no guarantees.

- If you buy a *New York Times* from a newsstand, it's reasonable to expect that beyond the front page will be articles written for that particular newspaper, and not articles appearing in the most recent edition of *Glamour* magazine. And you can reasonably expect that you will receive the paper in its entirety. Conversely, if you pick up a pile of newspapers at your local coffeehouse after someone has thumbed through, it would not be reasonable to assume that your favorite column will still be there. The person before you may have taken that part with him, or maybe that part had never been left on the table to begin with because the paper belonged to a previous owner who only left behind the sections he'd already read.

- If you leave for work on time and take a route you usually use and there's no reports of any traffic issues between your home and your workplace, it's reasonable to assume you'll probably arrive at your workplace at the time you had anticipated. Conversely, if you leave later than you normally do, make an extra stop to get some cash from the ATM and you get caught in a traffic jam, it's not at all reasonable to expect that you'll arrive on time to your workplace.

These examples may seem silly, but believe me, if you're in drama queen mode, your sense of reason can go right out the window. So don't brush off these kinds of examples too hastily as something you can't relate to.

As you can see, whenever possible, expectations should be flexible, kept at a minimum, and fitting to the reality of a situation. And in order to minimize drama queen reactions, your expectations should shift according to any changes in the context of a scenario, taking into account things like previous experience, how many people are involved (usually the more people, the more complicated a situation), what type of people they are, how much control you have, how much is in the hands of nature or other people, how much information you have on the front end, how reliable is the information source, and so forth.

I know this isn't easy to grasp, but I'm pretty sure that you'll become better and better at regulating your expectations the more you simply slow down and allow yourself to become aware of whatever they are, and then practice lowering the bar (especially when your expectations involve things over which you don't have full control). But, whatever you

Changing Your Expectations

do, don't lower your expectations so much that you allow yourself to be mistreated by others. Setting healthy boundaries is as important as being aware of your expectations.

Before we move on to changing expectations through adopting a thriver mentality, make a commitment to pay closer attention to your expectations on a regular basis. In fact, each time you embark on a new activity or interaction, ask yourself "What am I expecting from (x, y, or z,)?" And keep in mind these two quotes from a couple of friends of mine as I think they'll really help you put expectations in better perspective. One friend so aptly said, "Expectations are resentments under construction." And another friend of mine said of resentments: "Holding on to resentments is like swallowing poison, and then waiting for the other guy to die." Now *that's* dramatic.

Developing a Thriver Mentality

While understanding the differences between unreasonable and reasonable expectations is a very important step toward actually changing your expectations, drama queens also need to work on their overall mentality. In other words, in order to fully change our expectations, we have to leave all remnants of a victim or survivor mentality behind and adopt a *thriver* mentality instead. Otherwise, with a victim or survivor mentality, the intensity and the severity of the drama queen syndrome will increase and a vicious cycle will ensue. Hence, you can't possibly learn to lighten up and go with the flow. Thus, it is so important that you become a *thriver*; that is, someone who takes responsibility for your own actions and reactions and the choices you make. (More on this in a moment.)

If you've read any of my other books, you'll know that understanding the differences among victims, survivors, and thrivers is a common thread and emphasis throughout all of my writings. And because I believe wholeheartedly that our overall mentality toward the world has such a profound impact on our identity and our behavior, it's certainly worth revisiting. Plus, it never hurts to have a bit of a refresher course in something that can affect every area of your life. Rest assured, though I haven't gone into this topic with as much detail as in my previous book, *Healing the Sensitive Heart,* hopefully there's enough information here for you to fully grasp what it takes to become a thriver and hence have yet another tool to keep expectations in the healthy range.

If you're new to this concept, please pay extra close attention to the following section. Without a doubt, it is our core way of thinking that determines how we perceive the world, which, in turn, directly affects how we respond to the curve balls we receive. So, while I hope many aspects of this book benefit you, if you take away nothing else from it other than a new understanding of the *value* of leaving behind a victim or survivor mentality, then you will have gotten a lot. Now, let's examine this concept more closely, starting with victims and victim mentality.

There are many situations in life that would render someone a true victim, particularly during our early childhood years when we have so little choice about what happens to us. In other words, during certain developmental periods when we are dependent on others for our care, we can become victimized most easily, especially if those on whom we depend fail to meet our needs, or worse yet, actively abuse us. Here are some of the many examples of situations where someone would truly be considered a victim.

- Young children who are completely dependent on others for their care and whose caregivers abuse, neglect, or abandon them (or even threaten to do so). (Note: although adolescents are technically still legally considered minors and their guardians are held responsible for their actions, teenagers have far more choices and options in life, even if they're in a bad situation at home, than do young children.)
- Elderly or dependent adults who truly can't take care of themselves

because of some mental or physical condition and whose caregivers abuse, neglect, or abandon them.

- People who have never been granted the rights of freedom and independence, such as those who are raised in a country run by a dictator or whose rights of freedom and independence have been taken away by an institution or person in power.
- People whose rights of freedom and independence have been taken away temporarily, such as someone who gets held up at gunpoint, raped, and/or physically assaulted by someone of greater strength or who carries a weapon.
- People who get pummeled by a disaster, such as losing a home during a hurricane, getting hit by a drunk driver and losing a limb, or losing a loved one during a terrorist attack.

Now, mind you, I'm certainly not taking this lightly. Clearly millions and millions of people, if not billions, qualify as a victim because of one or more of these conditions at one or more times in their lives. But this is not the norm for most people living in the free countries throughout the world. (Plus, unfortunately for those whose rights are violated, they're not likely to ever be able to even get their hands on a book like this. But, hopefully that will change someday.) Also, even children who grew up in violent and abusive homes eventually become adults who can move out, move on, and create a healthy life for themselves. Hence, hardly any of these people remain victims throughout their life span. And chances are, if someone repeatedly finds herself in situations where she is victimized and she doesn't meet any of the above criteria, it's highly likely that she is re-victimizing herself because she's stuck in victim mentality and continues to make poor choices, putting herself in harm's way. And she may not even recognize that she's doing the choosing.

In reality, most people, especially by the time they reach adulthood, rarely, if ever, meet the criteria for victim status. And, even though abuse is prevalent in our society, most people aren't being abused. Even for those adults in abusive relationships, many truly could get out of their situations safely, though understandably they may fear that they're permanently trapped.

Granted, many people feel that they got short-changed—that is, they feel that their caregivers failed to adequately meet their needs, but they certainly weren't abandoned, abused, or neglected. Yet, millions and millions of people walk the earth believing that they are controlled by others, that they don't have the ability to make choices of their own, and that every moment of their lives is determined by forces outside themselves. They live in a state of victim mentality—as if they're in a maximum security prison on death row. Yikes!

Clearly this is an extreme description. But I've worked with people who are truly convinced that they have no say-so in any situation in their lives. They're not crazy or delusional, and often they are quite functional. But when you scratch beneath the surface, you discover that they're firmly planted in the belief that they are merely puppets controlled by the strings of a cruel and ugly world. Sad, but true. And these people fail to recognize the fact that they do have choices.

Clearly, one can think of many scenarios where sometimes most, if not all, available options will be unpleasant, possibly even horrific. For instance, if your house catches on fire and you're in it, there's not a whole lot you can do, other than leave and watch your house burn down or refuse to leave, hence making a choice to die. (Mind you, I certainly wouldn't recommend anyone make the latter choice.) But this type of scenario is not a typical event in most people's lives.

People stuck in victim mentality also have considerable difficulty seeing the severity of situations as ranging in degree. Rather they tend to see the world in black and white only—either as a victim or a non-victim. For these folks, having a wallet stolen while they're not even in the same room as the thief may feel as if it's as traumatic and debilitating as being held hostage at gunpoint during a bank robbery.

People stuck in victim mentality act as if they're being persecuted by a cruel and unfair world and many haven't even endured any particular trauma or deprivation. Of course, some people with victim mentality would have qualified as a true victim at one point in their lives, but even though their traumas are long gone, they still live in the world feeling as though they're treated as having fewer rights than anyone else. Because of this, they stay entrenched in a never-ending war with the rest of the world, fighting for their fair share even when their rights aren't actually being restricted at all.

Granted, many situations where someone has been victimized can have long-lasting effects, as in the case of someone who develops post-traumatic stress disorder. But most situations that render us powerless don't have to have such a traumatic impact in the long run once someone gets out of the victimizing situation, that is, as long as she/he doesn't become stuck in victim mentality.

Take, for example, a woman who is raped in a parking lot during the middle of the day in an area that's considered safe—clearly a situation where she has been victimized. I doubt anyone would be surprised to discover that this woman might have a very hard time dealing with this trauma for months, if not years, to come, particularly since she had been completely blindsided by the event. After all, it's not as if she walked into the middle of a group of gang-bangers completely sober and asked them to violate her.

But now let's tweak this example a bit and have this woman become a rape victim as a result of saying "no" to a guy with whom she's already in the act of having intercourse and he doesn't stop until he climaxes. Mind you, I'm not talking legal definitions, or the right to say "NO" at any moment. We all have the *right* to change our minds. But, doesn't this woman have a little bit of responsibility for putting herself in this situation? Or what if he really didn't hear her or believe that she meant "no"?

I most definitely do not believe in blaming the victim, but in the above scenario, I think the boundaries are quite blurred. And I do think the woman in this situation needs to take some responsibility for this outcome, though certainly not for the actual rape (if he did actually hear her and disregarded her wishes). I am neither being mean nor do I lack compassion here. Instead, I'm making this point because without owning her part in putting herself in the situation to begin with, she will likely keep finding herself in these precarious positions and thereby perpetuate her belief that she's a victim, without even realizing that she has a great deal of control over what happens to her most of the time. In other words, this woman needs to take ownership of how she puts herself in potentially harmful situations.

While some people with victim mentality fall into deep shame holes believing that they deserved what they endured, many others develop the expectation that other people who aren't victims owe them emotional compensation for what they've endured. They expect special favors, they feel entitled to more than their fair share—and not because they think they're better than others. Rather, they simply believe they should have the slate evened out.

If this describes you, take a deep breath and refrain from self-blame. You probably don't even realize that there's another way to approach your life. But the good news is that victim mentality can definitely be reversed. And you can take a step toward becoming a thriver at this very moment, simply by acknowledging that *you* are perpetuating your victim status, and then by owning that *you* have the power to change your way of thinking. But before I get into how to adopt a thriver mentality and make yet another leap toward changing unrealistic expectations and saying good-bye to drama queen reactions, let's take a look at survivor mentality.

Of course, by pure definition of the word, anyone who makes it through a trauma alive qualifies as a survivor—which is definitely a step above being in the midst of actually being victimized or being stuck in victim mentality. Mind you, not all victims who survive their trauma adopt a survivor mentality. Rather, they still stay stuck in victim mentality. But for those fortunate enough to advance to survivor mentality, there is a greater sense of freedom, at least in some areas. In other words, unlike the victim who is trapped in a maximum security prison awaiting death row, those in survivor mentality hold on to some hope for parole.

Those who adopt survivor mentality clearly have a greater sense of empowerment than those who remain in victim mode. They tend to recognize some sense of responsibility for their own safety and survival and they don't tend to feel as entitled to more than their fair share of life's goodies as do those stuck in victim mentality. But, even with these improvements, survivors aren't totally free and they often blur the boundaries between where their personal responsibility starts and stops. They may have many moments where they can chill out and enjoy the moment, but these are often short lived. Also, this isn't an all or nothing process. In fact, many of those with survivor mentality may dive back into a victim mentality, especially when things don't go as planned. In general, however, mid-level drama queens tend to embrace a survivor mentality whereas those with high-level features tend to be more burdened by a victim mentality.

Chandra moved from victim to survivor mentality pretty quickly once she entered therapy and realized that there was more than one lens through which to view the world. She'd been a victim of molestation during her preteens and never got the help she needed at the time of discovery by her caregivers. Later on, during adolescence and through about age twenty-six, Chandra dealt with her repressed feelings of shame and anger by acting out sexually and by using drugs and alcohol. As is typical of young girls in her shoes, she got herself into many nasty situations where she became re-victimized. Clearly she was not responsible for the actual violations she suffered (which included having her car stolen, being sexually assaulted by a drug-addicted "friend," staying in abusive relationships), but she was responsible for taking charge of ending her cycle of putting herself in high-risk situations. Once she learned this, her drama queen syndrome and underlying victim mentality began to heal.

Unexpectedly however, after about a year or two of relative stability, Chandra was fired from her job because someone had spread rumors about her having a romantic relationship with a coworker. Though it wasn't her fault that people had misinterpreted her behavior, she had developed a reputation for being a flirt, and this behavior—while innocent enough—came back to haunt her. What Chandra hadn't noticed was that she was very attractive and some of the women she worked with were jealous of her and her sensuality. Some of the woman viewed her flirting with the guys in the office as a threat to their own egos because she was getting more attention than they were and a few of them sought out revenge by making up a rumor.

Rather than being able to understand the nature of office drama, Chandra took the events that transpired in her workplace as a personal assault and she spiraled back into victim mentality. She had unconsciously come to expect that other people shouldn't hold her accountable for her actions because she'd had such a rough life. Chandra's dark side of her drama queen syndrome reared its ugly head and she became very nasty toward her boss, actually resorting to threats of violence.

I'm certainly not suggesting that Chandra's employer was justified in firing her. And it would clearly have been appropriate for Chandra to defend herself in an assertive manner, possibly even pursuing a wrongful termination case. But I am suggesting that Chandra didn't need to react with such intensity and rage. And had she moved all the way toward a thriver mentality she would not have succumbed to her former victim mentality way of thinking. Thankfully, Chandra didn't act out her threats and this event helped her realize that it was high time she dump both the victim and survivor mentality and permanently adopt a thriver position, making it possible to eradicate her drama queen syndrome.

So, while people certainly can and do get victimized and hopefully survive, they don't have to stay stuck in a victim or survivor mentality. In fact, I hope you're getting the message that if you want to truly become serene and give up being a drama queen, you can no longer be beholden to victim or survivor mentality. Rather you must commit to adopting a thriver mentality.

Though thrivers all have unique features as individuals, they tend to share the following characteristics. Thrivers:

- usually enjoy life
- can find the silver lining in most situations no matter how traumatic
- recognize and fully accept what they have control over and what they don't
- don't waste time on trying to change situations where they don't have control
- set healthy boundaries with others and never tolerate abuse
- believe that life has many wonderful aspects and it's their job to find these
- live in the moment as often as is possible
- understand that people make mistakes
- don't personalize other people's responses unless they are actually personal
- don't get easily offended
- allow people to have their own opinions and thoughts without being offended
- can shake the little things off easily
- don't waste much time complaining
- accept responsibility for their own actions and their consequences, whether good or bad
- recognize that there are consequences to every action, sometimes good, sometimes not so good
- actively search out solutions using all resources available when there is a problem
- don't waste time feeling guilty when they haven't done anything wrong

The Solutions

- have a positive attitude most of the time
- don't dwell on the past or worry about the future
- enjoy being productive as well as tranquil and relaxed
- strive to minimize drama in their own lives
- continually develop flexible styles of responding to various situations, welcoming growth and change

Of course I could probably go on and on about other features associated with being a thriver but this list gives you a pretty good picture of how a thriver lives in the world. I know it's unrealistic to expect to be able to live in this mode 24/7, 365 days a year, for the rest of your life. But as long as you're not actively being victimized or in the middle of a true crisis or real danger, then there's no reason not to be able to live in this mode most of the time.

Now, before we move on to developing healthy core beliefs (the third step in being able to permanently change our expectations and minimize the drama queen syndrome) take a moment and reflect on your own mentality. Using the descriptions and examples above, try assessing where you fall on the continuum. And make efforts every day to adopt a thriver mentality. You'll be amazed at how quickly your unrealistic expectations will dissipate when you take responsibility for your own choices and behavior and accept that you are in charge of your life and your happiness.

Developing Healthy Core Beliefs

Becoming aware of your unreasonable expectations and adopting a thriver mentality will definitely put you on the right track for actually changing unrealistic expectations and ultimately to leaving behind the drama queen syndrome. However, in order to really make a mark, it's also very valuable to adopt healthy core beliefs about the world. Below is a list of beliefs which I have found to be very helpful in keeping the drama queen syndrome at bay. Of course, you may think of others that I've left out. So don't rule out your own ideas just because you may not see them included here.

As you go through these items, rate yourself on a scale of 0–4 with how much you agree or disagree with each of them.

I don't believe this at all: 0
I rarely believe this: 1
I sometimes believe this: 2
I frequently believe this: 3
I always believe this: 4

1. I'm responsible for my happiness.
2. I'm responsible for my actions.
3. I'm responsible for taking care of my needs whenever possible and asking for the help I need when I'm unable to meet them, all the while understanding that some people I ask may not agree to help me and that I may have to go elsewhere.
4. I believe there are differences between needs and preferences.
5. I'm responsible for being respectful of other people's needs and feelings.
6. I can control my own feelings and actions.
7. I cannot control the feelings and actions of others. (Though as parents or caregivers of dependent individuals, we do have the power to control others to some extent. And this is a huge responsibility that should never be exploited.)
8. No one is responsible for making up for anything I didn't get in childhood from my caregivers. (Note: if you were neglected or abused, you may desire that your abusers accept responsibility for their behavior, but you can't make them be accountable. As a result, if you wait for such an event for you to move on, you're going to

stay stuck most likely for a very long time, since people who mistreat others very rarely acknowledge what they've done.)

9. I need to let people know what I'm thinking and feeling (respectfully, of course) and not expect others to be able to read my mind.

10. I accept that people are responsible for their own lives and that I am at best on an equal playing field, but more likely secondary to someone else.

11. If someone else is putting my needs first (and I'm not in a true victim position), then I do my best not to exploit this person's emotional generosity. (I don't have to take responsibility for this person's possible codependency, but I try very hard not to allow the person to exploit himself by taking more than my fair share.)

12. I enjoy being in the driver's seat of my life.

13. I enjoy helping other people in need as long as I continue to replenish my own needs on a regular basis.

14. I believe I should behave ethically and morally.

15. I believe I should think through the consequences of my actions and always do my best to minimize harm to myself or others.

16. I believe that living a balanced life includes relatively equal proportions of play, rest, and productivity and is the best way to live.

17. I am responsible for setting good boundaries with others and not allow people to treat me like a doormat (nor do I treat others as one).

18. I would rather opt for calmness over chaos.

19. I can be content in quiet times and at ease in high energy situations because I choose the balance of these energies.

20. I can shake off a bad day or a difficult moment most of the time (barring a real crisis or emergency).

21. I feel enriched by the adversity I've endured in my life, not a victim to it.

22. I'm not easily offended by others people's behavior (unless of course it's outlandish, violent, or appalling to anyone who is human).

23. I don't get my feelings hurt easily because I know I'm responsible for my feelings and if I don't like something I'm involved in I find appropriate ways to get out of it.
24. My identity is defined by my successes, not by my hardships.
25. I'm comfortable allowing other people to be in the limelight.

Now add up your score. This exercise is simply meant to be a quick assessment tool, so don't take your score too seriously. Again, none of the scales in this book have been scientifically validated. Roughly speaking, the higher your score, the more likely your core beliefs will help you decrease unreasonable expectations and help you thrive. Be careful that you didn't inflate your score; otherwise you may miss some important information about yourself and what you need to work on to achieve your ultimate goal of being able to lighten up and go with the flow.

Actually, I would doubt that you would have a very high score at this point, unless you started out as a very low-level drama queen. In any case, I recommend you keep this tool handy. And as you go through the other exercises in the book and practice putting them into action, go back and reassess yourself on this scale from time to time to see whether you're making progress in adopting healthy core beliefs and minimizing any unrealistic expectations.

In order to further increase your advancement in developing healthy core beliefs, using the above list of twenty-five items, make a new list for yourself ranking the items from your lowest score to those where you rated yourself a four. In other words, put all your 1s first, then your 2s, then 3s, and lastly, your 4s. If you don't have any 4s at this time, don't worry, you will soon enough (if you diligently practice and apply all the tools in this book). Then rewrite each item so that it becomes the statement you actually currently believe. For instance, if you rated yourself a one on "#12) I enjoy being in the driver's seat of my life" then the counterstatement to reflect your rating would be something like: "I don't enjoy being in the driver's seat of my life" or "I don't believe I can be the driver of my life." Once you've made your counterstatements that reflect where you currently stand try the following steps:

Step One: Starting with your 1s, try to figure out where and how you ended up with your belief. If you can't give it a context, then let that go and move on to the next step. If you can, then write a couple of notes to yourself so you can remember how this belief came about.

Step Two: Next, pick one of the items on your list where you rated yourself a 1, and start practicing the healthy belief instead. For instance, let's say you rated yourself a 1 on item #23 ("I don't get my feelings hurt easily because I know I'm responsible for my feelings and if I don't like something I'm involved in I find appropriate ways to get out of it"), then your current belief would be something like: "My feelings are easily hurt and I believe other people make me feel the way I do. I don't have any control over my feelings and I stay in situations where I allow others to continue to hurt my feelings." But rather than give this negative belief any more power, go out each day for the next week and practice setting better boundaries with people and building a thicker skin. You don't have to lose your sensitivity. Rather, you just need to learn when to show it and when it's better kept under wraps.

Step Three: Once you've gone through all your 1s, then move on to the 2s and then the 3s. You don't have to conquer this all in one day. Remember, this is a learning process that takes time and effort. It's not an immunization shot in the arm.

Way to go! Now we can move on to learning how to put feelings in perspective.

Chapter 7

Putting Your Feelings into Perspective

Our capacity to feel and express our emotions is fundamental to our essence. Feelings make us come alive and distinguish us from other life forms, especially from our mechanical creations like computers, iPods, and cell phones. Plus, the variation among our feelings and our ability to express these complexities through multiple avenues (body language, words, scents) continues to increase through our evolution. And, I don't know about you, but I think life would be incredibly boring and robotic were it not for our capacity to experience the full range of our emotions. However, while I think that most people would probably agree with me concerning the importance of our emotional lives, drama queens often go overboard in this area, giving far too much weight to their feelings. For drama queens, emotions frequently dominate, often leaving rational thoughts out of the picture entirely. And, should anyone get in the way of a drama queen's colorful display of emotions, look out.

Drama queens cling to their feelings like a mother would cling to her son heading off to war in a third world country where she may never see him again. Yes, that sounds a little "dramatic." But all kidding aside drama queens do tend to give far too much importance to their feelings, often believing that they would not be who they are without them. I'm not saying that as a drama queen that you should strive to eliminate your feelings to the level of one of those zombies you might see in a horror movie. Quite the contrary, we all should value feelings very much. But, as a drama queen, you're likely to experience your emotional world as being on automatic pilot without you having any control over them. Remember, nothing I say is meant to be shaming. But in order to create a more serene existence and improve your quality of life, you have to face this reality.

If your emotions rule your world, you're probably not aware that you actually have complete say-so in how your feelings come about, what you're feeling, and how much intensity you actually give to any one emotion. And at this point, you may not even realize that you have *any* control over your feelings, let alone the ability to fully take charge of your emotional world. But ideally, you will soon learn that you have the power to raise your contentment level and peace of mind at will, without even having to go to magic school.

So, rest assured. Nothing in this chapter or in this entire book will inhibit your capacity to feel your emotions as intensely as you desire. On the contrary. You will retain all of your inherent abilities, but you'll actually come to decide *what* to feel, *when* to feel, and *how* you will express your emotions. Quite frankly, as I hope you're beginning to understand, some things just aren't worth all the fuss, especially not if it leads to a lot of stress and aggravation.

Since you want to subdue the drama queen in you, you will benefit greatly by learning how to buffer your feelings with reality-based thoughts and how to stop giving so much power to your emotions. My goal is three-fold: (1) to teach you how to embrace your feelings, (2) to show you how to stay in charge of *choosing* what you feel, and (3) to give you guidelines for how you can consciously, rather than impulsively, select the actions you take as a result of how you feel. In other words, you will learn how to permanently take over the driver's seat of your emotional world and no longer be the passenger in a runaway train wreck. Of course, you may slip up now and again (I certainly do), but at least you'll be able to get back in charge more easily and without too much wreckage from your detours.

You might also be worried that you will lose your ability to entertain people through your flair. After all, one of the common very well-liked characteristics of many lovable drama queens is their ability to make other people laugh (at their own expense sometimes) and to be the life of the party. Many achieve their popularity through exaggerations and embellishments, and drama queens are typically very good story-tellers. But again, nothing in the pages that follow or those you've already read will diminish your capacity to keep alive whatever you desire. Rather, all the information, tools, and tips are simply aimed at keeping you *conscious* and *choiceful*. Plus, while a drama queen's flair and flamboyance can be so delightful, at times he or she may go overboard and defeat its endearing purpose. Hence, you'll want to pay close attention to the section at the end of this chapter which will help you learn to differentiate harmful exaggerations from harmless ones.

First, let's start with a basic rundown of what feelings/emotions actually are.

Feelings

I was contemplating how to address this topic and thought it would be fun to simply look up the definition of *feeling*. I certainly could have come up with a definition of my own, as I'm sure you can as well. But I opted to check out a more formal description. And, while I had expected to find a simple, two or three phrase, definition, I was surprised to see so many variations just from pressing the *look up* function on Microsoft Word. Here's what I found from *Encarta Dictionary*: English (North America):

"Feeling (noun): (1) sense of touch: the sensation felt on touching something (2) ability to have physical sensation: the ability to perceive physical sensation in a part of the body (3) something experienced physically or mentally: a perceived physical or mental sensation (4) something felt emotionally: a perceived emotional state (5) affection: the emotional response of love, sympathy, or tenderness toward somebody (6) ability to express emotion: the capacity to experience strong emotions (7) impression sensed: a particular impression, appearance, effect, or atmosphere sensed from something (8) instinctive awareness . . . or presentiment of something (9) instinctive understanding or talent (10) expressive ability."

Go figure. Who would think you could find ten different ways to define the simple word—*feeling*? Of course on closer inspection there's a lot of overlap among the ten descriptions. Nevertheless, this gives you a sense of just how important our feelings are since there are so many nuances just for the word itself. And that doesn't even cover the varieties of feelings.

When you think about all the words we have to describe our feelings or emotions it seems as if we have as many variations to our feelings as there are brands of cereal on the supermarket shelves, maybe even more. Sometimes we experience a single feeling, like sad or mad. In other moments we experience elaborate combo packs, with a mixture of something like fear plus sad plus annoyed plus ashamed. (What emotion would you call that?) Sometimes we can articulate our feelings very clearly, sometimes we're confused about what they are and the only thing we can differentiate is between whether we feel "good" or "bad." Sometimes we use vague terms to say how we feel which could mean different things to different people like when we say, "I'm upset." But "upset" could mean angry to one person, hurt to another, or disappointed to yet another person.

Feelings can flip-flop quickly and also range in intensity. At one moment you might be mostly happy but a tad bit sad. Or you might feel angry at someone and then feel happy a moment later if the person says something funny and makes you laugh, only to then again return to being mad because you realize you're still offended by something she said earlier.

As long as feelings are acknowledged, embraced, and given appropriate expression, they are usually very fleeting and fluid. True, a particular feeling may remain relatively constant if the event which inspired the feeling in the first place continues on. For instance, if one of your favorite relatives is dying of cancer, you're likely going to be in a state of grieving even though she hasn't yet passed away. You'll likely run the full gamut of emotions, possibly dominated by sadness. But since you're living as a *thriver*, not stuck in the drama queen syndrome, you will still be able to feel joy and other emotions simultaneously because your life is still happening, despite your relative's disease. In essence, the world doesn't stop because someone is dying; nor does your life end either. You still deserve to have other ongoing experiences. And continuing to allow yourself to enjoy life doesn't make you cold-hearted or callous.

Sometimes people judge or repress their feelings if they've categorized them as bad—seeking the good ones more often and avoiding the bad ones whenever possible. But we all don't include the same feelings into categories of good or bad. For example, some people might only put happy feelings in the good category and all others in the bad category whereas others may only put anger or fear in the bad category. Our upbringing, cultural mores, the media, and gender stereotyping can all influence how we categorize feelings and which ones we're most comfortable expressing. For instance, if you're a guy influenced by the American culture, you may have been taught that anger is good and fear is bad. Conversely, if you're female, you may have been socialized to believe that all feelings associated with anger are bad when expressed by a girl, but that it's fine to express sadness, happiness, or fear.

Some people judge certain feelings very harshly and don't allow themselves to express these in particular, but they're comfortable expressing those feelings they deem as acceptable. Some feel very vulnerable when they experience certain emotions and they believe they are strengthened by other feelings. Some people were shamed for expressing any feelings at all. Hence they become potential volcanoes ready to erupt at any moment with emotional lava. Oh, what a mess they can make. (I've certainly made some of these messes along my life's journey!)

Some people prefer to keep their feeling language simple, covering only the core basics, including mad, sad, glad, and afraid. Others like to use the hundreds of fancy names we have for emotions, each one reflecting a slightly different combination of the basics, similar to an artist blending and mixing all the primary colors and creating a tapestry of art.

Many people confuse thoughts for feelings. They often miss out on the beauty of experiencing or expressing any true feelings. For instance, have you or have you ever heard someone say something like, "I feel like you're avoiding me." Well if you break this down, you'll see that there is no feeling expressed here at all—only a statement of observation. In other words, it would be a more accurate statement to say, "I perceive that you are avoiding me and I feel _____ (fill in the blank with an emotion)." I can recall many times in my life where I've actually been happy that someone appears to be avoiding me because I wasn't necessarily in the right place mentally to deal with that someone.

If I hear someone say, "I feel *like* . . ." or "I feel *that* . . ." then I'm pretty sure I'm not going to hear anything about what the person is actually feeling, but rather what he or she is thinking. Now that's not to say that this person doesn't actually have feelings in that moment, but just that the emotion is not being communicated.

Now just for fun, using the idea that sometimes feelings get camouflaged by thoughts or perceptions, see if you can pick out the feeling imposters in the list below. Hint: there are seven of them.

Putting Your Feelings into Perspective

1. exhaustion
2. frustration
3. pain
4. jealousy
5. inclusiveness
6. tranquility
7. agitation
8. rejection
9. loneliness
10. boredom
11. aloneness
12. worry
13. happiness
14. interrogation
15. criticism
16. bashfulness
17. guardedness
18. confusion
19. sadness
20. elation

Check out what you came up with. Those that I would put in the perception or thought category, as opposed to the emotional category, are: *inclusiveness, rejection, aloneness, interrogation, criticism, guardedness,* and *confusion.* I know. People commonly use these words when they believe they're making a feeling statement. But let me explain why I don't.

First off, "inclusiveness" is actually an observation of whether you are part of something, but it still doesn't name what you feel. You could actually be just as happy to be excluded from something as to be included, depending upon what it is. For instance, if you dread a group of coworkers at the office and they include you in their clan by inviting you out on a Friday evening for happy-hour drinks, you might be annoyed, irritated, or worried about how to say "no" without creating awkwardness. Then again, if you enjoy this group of coworkers you would likely be happy to have been included. Similarly, the counterpart, "rejection," is also commonly used to describe a feeling. But actually it is also an observation or an interpretation of an action that has been taken. So if you perceive you've been rejected, the next step is to ask yourself how you feel about it.

"Aloneness" is also an observation of a state you're in but says nothing about how you feel. You very well may be alone and be quite content about it. Yet, if you don't like being alone and you are, you might feel afraid, or sad, or lonely. Then again, you might not be alone at all but you sense that you are disconnected from everyone around you, and hence, you feel lonely.

"Interrogation" and "criticism" also do not convey the emotion attached to the observation or perception of someone's action toward you. Granted most people don't like to be interrogated, but for very open and curious people, the process may not be that bad at all. And sometimes criticisms can feel good if they're constructive and presented well. Likewise, someone who says "I feel guarded" also is not conveying an emotion but rather information about her state of openness. I'd want to know what feelings the guard is there to protect. "Confusion" also isn't a feeling. Rather, it conveys a state of being. Sometimes people are perfectly content in a state of confusion, at other times possibly frightened or even angry, depending upon the context.

I don't mean to sound nit-picky, but I just want you to start paying closer attention to the language you use to express your emotions (both with yourself and toward others). To get your butt firmly planted in the driver's seat of your life requires being able to identify and differentiate among all the feelings. If you believe you're naming your feelings, but you're actually naming a thought or observing an action, then your feelings won't actually get the healthy airtime they deserve and that's when trouble is bound to occur. In other words, if you don't clearly understand your feelings, you'll likely express them through unhealthy actions. And if you don't even know what you're expressing, then you can't possibly put your feelings into perspective.

Jan, a mother of two boys in her late thirties, came to therapy to deal with her pending divorce from Rick, her husband of fourteen years. Sadly, neither Jan nor Rick understood Jan's drama queen syndrome. He wanted a tranquil and happy home, and she did too—but she couldn't seem to help herself from stirring the pot even when things were going well between them. Actually sometimes she created drama, *especially* when things were going well between them. After thirteen years of weathering what felt like a class five hurricane and repeated efforts to get her to seek help, Rick ultimately filed for divorce. Needless to say, this sent Jan into an even deeper state of agitation and emotional turmoil. She begged and pleaded with him to give her another chance. But he'd heard her pleas so many times before, and she'd never followed through with her promises to change. Hence, he simply couldn't risk opening up his heart to her anymore.

One of Jan's biggest hurdles to overcoming her drama queen syndrome involved dealing with her feelings. Jan being a very sensitive and emotional person had grown up in a family full of stoics. That might not have been such a bad thing, except that Jan was either teased or harshly reprimanded anytime she dared to show any emotion other than contentment. Tears of sadness were simply not tolerated and gosh forbid she would show any signs of anger. Forced to keep bottling up her emotions, Jan failed to learn a healthy model of expressing herself. She would hide in her bedroom, under her covers, and sometimes sob for hours and hours on end. Other times she would swallow her emotions and entirely deny their existence. By the time she reached adulthood, she was a ticking time bomb with her emotions on the verge of erupting at even the tiniest of things.

Her relationship with Rick had started out with a lot of fireworks, steamy chemistry, and tons of laughter. They fell madly in love and shared many great times throughout the first year or so. But as Jan became more invested in the relationship, rather than becoming more secure, she actually became more and more insecure. And sadly, she was never able to fully experience and hold on to Rick's love for her.

Rick was leery about marrying Jan, but she convinced him that making that commitment would give her the assurance she needed to settle into the relationship. No such luck. Actually, the opposite happened. She felt threatened by everything he did, unless he was exclusively focused and doting on her. Initially, Rick talked himself into believing that her dramatic moments were the result of her insecurities and he believed through his consistent demonstrations of love that he could put these to rest with time. But, her emotional outbursts only got worse, especially once they had their children.

Rick made several efforts to help Jan mellow out and enjoy their lives together. He tried to soothe her insecurities through reassurance and other gestures of kindness and concern. He wanted back the joyful gal that he had fallen in love with. But now the joy was rarely seen, replaced by volatility and extreme reactions to minor upsets. To make matters worse, Jan blamed Rick for her emotional volatility and wouldn't take any responsibility for it herself.

Jan wasn't a bad person. She simply wasn't able to see that she played a very big part in creating problems in their relationship; that is, by blowing things completely out of proportion, she continually put undue strain on their marriage. For instance, if Rick were to come home even a half an hour later than expected, she would become instantly enraged and accuse him of all sorts of destructive things like having an affair, not loving or caring about her, and so forth. She would lash out at him and storm around for days. But because Jan wasn't receptive to taking responsibility for how her emotional outbursts were affecting Rick, he eventually just got sick and tired of trying to appease her. He didn't know what else to do but leave her. When he finally threw in the towel, rather than seeing that she'd played a very significant role in why he left her, instead

Putting Your Feelings into Perspective

Jan convinced herself that she should have seen this coming all along and never should have married him in the first place.

Fortunately, though Jan wasn't able to save her marriage, she finally saw that she needed some help when one of her friends confronted her one day and told her that she wasn't a victim in her marriage. Her friend actually put it to her quite bluntly by telling Jan that it was actually her fault that her marriage ended. Thankfully, Jan didn't turn her back on her friend, but instead found her way to my office.

Jan's response to her childhood wound was to vow never again to be put in a position where she would have to censor her feelings. By golly, she believed she had a right to express her feelings any way she wanted. And sadly, without her knowing it, she was displacing years and years worth of unexpressed emotion onto Rick. He was paying the price for her having been so censored as a kid. Granted, Rick certainly wasn't a saint, but it seemed like he was a pretty good guy and Jan was clearly misperceiving many of his actions as being uncaring. Jan came to learn that because she had been taught to repress her feelings she had never learned how to handle her emotions when they would arise. She also came to eventually understand that her feelings didn't have to be so powerful. Most importantly, she learned that she could contain her negative feelings by slowing down and re-processing whatever it was that she was reacting to. In essence, she learned the fundamental lesson that feelings result from perception. Hence, she grew to appreciate that she could change many of her feelings simply by examining her perception of an event.

Now let's get down to the nitty gritty of how those little buggers (our feelings) come about and how you, like Jan, can learn to put them into perspective.

The Solutions

Perception, Thoughts, and Emotions

Feelings don't just happen to us. Rather they result from our perceptions, observations, and/or thoughts about whatever is happening at any given moment, has already happened, or what we contemplate might happen in the future. And because our emotions are directly linked to our perceptions and thoughts, we can alter the course of our emotions by fine-tuning our observation skills and becoming more aware of the meanings we ascribe to individual events. Hence, if you want to become more serene you need to start paying closer attention to your perceptions and be willing to acknowledge that sometimes your interpretations might be skewed and distorted. And then you need to be willing to ascribe a different meaning to the event. As I've stated already throughout the book, drama queens notoriously put a negative spin on many events that are simply neutral, benign, or possibly even positive. It's critical to put your feelings into a context and not jump to as many conclusions.

Before I explain further, here's a simple exercise for you to try. Below are some scenarios grouped in pairs. Within each pair is the exact same event. But each has a different assumption or meaning attached to the event. I'd like you to read the first item in each pair, and ask yourself how you think you'd feel. Then read the second item in the pair and see whether the alternative context changes how you think you'd feel. Keep in mind that there is no wrong or right answer. This is merely an exercise in increasing your awareness and attention to the context within which you experience emotion. So here goes.

Scenario 1.a. Imagine someone you care for very deeply forgets to call you on your birthday. He or she has always remembered your birthday in the past, and you've made it crystal clear that birthdays are very important to you. Let's say that you assume he forgot—how do you think you'd feel?

Scenario 1.b. Now imagine that you assume he didn't forget but rather that something must have come up for *him* that got in the way of calling you. Now how do you think you'd feel?

Scenario 2. a. Your boss calls you into a meeting at the end of your workday. You believe he's taking advantage of you and not respecting that you have obligations outside of work and shouldn't be asked to stay late. How do you think you'd feel?

Scenario 2. b. Your boss calls you to the meeting and you assume he's going to tell you about the promotion you're up for. Now how do you think you'd feel?

Scenario 3. a. Your best friend doesn't invite you to a dinner party she's throwing. You assume you've been dissed and that she's mad at you for something. How do you think you'd feel?

Scenario 3. b. You don't get the invite but you find out that she's only having people over who have expressed an interest in funding a new project she's developing (you haven't expressed any interest). How do you think you'd feel?

Scenario 4. a. Your mother tells you she thinks you're burning the candle at both ends and she's worried about you. How would you perceive her intentions and how would you feel?

Scenario 4. b. Mom says the same thing but you have always experienced her as someone who criticizes and picks on you for your choices. Would this change how you might respond?

Scenario 5. a. A driver of another car bumps into you at a stop sign, leaving you with a fender bender. You didn't see him approaching your bumper because you were looking straight ahead, not in your rearview mirror. How would you feel?

Scenario 5. b. The same driver hits your car but you can also see that he was on his cell phone while he was making his stop. Any change in emotion?

Now using the same scenarios above, contemplate a few alternative contexts for each of them and see whether you would have any more changes in how you think you'd feel.

The Solutions

You may or may not have thought that you would react differently based on the change of context, but chances are you noticed at least subtle differences. In any event, in order to decrease the drama queen syndrome it's important that you take into account the context of something that inspires feelings. As a rule of thumb, I recommend that with regards to your relationships with people you should try to ascribe neutral or benign intentions to someone's behavior, unless you have strong evidence to the contrary. For instance, unless you have repeated experiences with someone who has shown ill will or malicious motives in her actions toward you, then if she does something that bugs you, try not to conclude that she intended to hurt you.

David perceived his girlfriend, Nancy, as being lazy. This caused him to have serious reservations about whether or not he should marry her, since he placed a very high value on productivity. Though David tended to be only a low-level drama queen, whenever he interpreted Nancy's actions as stemming from laziness, he would get really bent out of shape, sometimes actually becoming very demeaning toward her. As it turns out, what David perceived as laziness (and as a result being continually disappointed in her) was really inaccurate. In actuality, Nancy was probably as busy as David. But David didn't value all the things she was doing, hence he wasn't keeping track of or valuing many of her contributions to the relationship. Once he recognized this misperception and misinterpretation of her behavior, his feelings changed and he saw her in a new light.

Sometimes our feelings come about because of our own internal thought process about something that isn't happening in the immediate moment. For instance, you may find yourself angry and irritable without really realizing why. But if you stop and think about it for a bit, you might realize you're still upset about something that happened a few days ago when you perceived that you had been slighted. Sadly, some people hold on to negative feelings over things that happened years, if not decades, ago. But it's not good to hold on to old feelings; no matter how justified you may believe you are. Even if someone has wronged you and never took responsibility for his actions, it's still time to let go of old emotional wounds. Otherwise they remain just below the surface, ready to be ignited by any little strike.

Our bodies operate best when we simply acknowledge what we feel at any given moment, understand the context in which we feel it (with as minimal distortion as possible), determine whether an action is required, put the action into effect if there is one warranted, and then move on. Yes—it's far easier said then done. Nevertheless, this is a good model to start practicing when working on putting your feelings into perspective.

The key is that you don't have to feel any particular emotion based on an event. While your initial internal reactions and feelings may be difficult to control, especially if you've linked together or have associated certain events with particular feelings, you can do a lot to move your feelings toward emotions of your choosing by being conscious of what it is you're reacting to. To a large extent you can actually achieve "being happy anyway" most of the time.

Here's what I mean. Barring any life or death situations which we already covered in Chapter Five, you can break the associations you have linked between events and feelings. Again I can't give you an all-inclusive list since every moment in life elicits different feelings (even if we're not attending to them). But here are a couple of commonly associated events and corresponding feelings:

1. If someone expresses anger toward you, you may become defensive and angry, and believe you must retaliate.
2. If someone starts to cry, you may become concerned and experience more tender feelings.
3. If someone verbally threatens you, you may drop into fight-flight-freeze mode and act purely out of instinct.
4. If someone gives you a piece of unsolicited criticism, you may become angry or hurt.

5. If someone tells a joke and you think it's funny, you may laugh and experience happy feelings.
6. If someone brings you a gift you like, you may feel loved.

Notice how for each of these, I said "may" instead of "will" lead to whatever feeling. That's because, depending upon your life experience, your interpretation of the meaning of these events, and/or your particular experience with a person, you may have very different emotional responses than the ones I listed. The point, once again, is simply that you recognize that you're not a puppet on a string. Rather you can *decide* how to feel. In other words, taking #1, you don't have to become defensive and angry toward someone who is mad at you. Instead, you could stay neutral and get curious about why she is upset. Upon discovery, you might actually feel sad that your friend spent time angry at you because *she'd* misinterpreted something you had said.

To summarize this section, keep in mind the following points:

- Feelings have no "wrong" or "right" to them so you should never try to argue yourself or anyone out of his or her feelings. However, perception does often have more of a flavor of right and wrong and the more something gets distorted the more chance we have of having corresponding feelings that won't serve us well.
- Feelings can change if we recognize our misperceptions and then revise our thinking according to reality. And if you discover you haven't misperceived anything and your feelings are warranted, you can still choose to let the feelings go by taking action to remedy whatever has upset you (which, by the way, sometimes means doing absolutely nothing except for acknowledging the feeling to your own self).
- Feelings should be acknowledged and embraced, but not given the power to rule our decisions about our actions.
- Feelings don't determine how we should react to them—we have

to consciously make that choice. For instance, being angry doesn't require hitting someone or lashing out.

- We function best when we let our feelings have airtime but still remain connected to rational thinking.
- We are responsible for our own feelings—people do not *make* us feel anything. Rather, we choose our own feelings based on how we perceive a situation.

Expressing Emotion

The third puzzle piece to putting feelings into perspective involves paying attention to how you actually express your feeling outwardly. This is largely where drama queens get into trouble in their relationships with others. While feelings are never right or wrong (they just are), how we behave as a result of our feelings definitely requires some guidelines. Otherwise, we'd be running around like cavemen and women beating each other over the head with our clubs whenever we don't like something or believe we deserve to have something that someone else has. So while it's important to embrace your feelings, it's equally important to learn how to consciously, rather than impulsively, select the actions you take as a result of how you feel.

Regardless of how your drama queen syndrome developed, it's still your responsibility to be accountable for your actions. You're not entitled to behave any way you like with no consequences, even if you were cheated, deprived, or victimized at any point in your life. And while most people become self-righteous and indignant when they believe they've been wronged, still, no one has license to fly off the handle in a tirade or tizzy fit. Even positive overreactions can have negative results and need to be monitored to some extent as well. For example, if you're raising your own children, you're probably aware that it's developmentally important for them to be able to have their own feelings and not constantly get upstaged by others. Similarly, within an intimate relationship, if one partner is constantly hogging the limelight because of her high emotional energy and reactivity, the relationship will usually suffer.

"So how do I express my emotions appropriately?" you might be asking. Well I think you'll be on a pretty good path if you follow these ten guidelines below:

1. Always keep in mind that your actions have consequences, whatever they may be.

2. You always have the right to express your feelings to yourself, though I still recommend that you do so respectfully.

3. You are ultimately responsible for soothing and healing your own feelings and generating your own happiness.

4. If you do decide to express your feeling to others, you need to be respectful of other people's boundaries. If someone doesn't want to hear what you have to say, then you shouldn't try to coerce, manipulate, or force him to listen.

5. Your feelings should not upstage or take precedence over someone else's needs, nor should they take precedence over your needs.

6. If someone is treating you badly, you can always leave the interaction or the relationship. But I caution you to first examine your perception of their behavior and put it in context because you may sometimes discover that what you thought was so bad, wasn't so bad at all.

7. Practice the art of self-soothing on a routine basis.

8. Give people space and time to process your feelings when you do express them. Not everyone is equipped with healthy tools for handling emotions. If you press upon others too forcefully they're likely to push you away.

9. Try to make "I" statements when expressing emotions to someone, particularly if you're expressing your feelings based on an interaction with him or her. In other words, if someone's behavior pisses

you off or frightens you, say something with this format: "I perceive that you did (such and such) and I feel (name the feeling)." For instance, "It seems like you don't want to spend time with me because you've been working late every night and I feel sad about that."

10. Most important, try to be curious about other people's behavior and the intentions behind them, rather than jump to conclusions about what you believe the meaning or motive to be. In other words, be careful not to write an entire script in your own head without checking with the other person for its accuracy, or you may very well be wrong.

Keep in mind that these guidelines are particularly important when it comes to expressing the emotions most people would consider to be negative, like anger, frustration, disappointment, etc. But, even if we ascribe positive intentions and develop happy feelings about the impact of someone's behavior, we could still end up in a drama queen funk. For instance, let's say you're dating a new guy and he brings you flowers on the second date. You may think, "Man, this guy really must like me." Then of course, if you like him, you'll start creating all kinds of positive scenarios about your future together. Lo and behold, he cancels the next date, and you never hear from him again. Oy vey—the drama queen in you is *not* going to be pleased. Hence, I suggest you use these guidelines whenever your emotions flare and you're looking for an avenue to express them.

Emotions don't always need to be expressed to other people. Pets often serve up a nice listening ear (but don't yell at them). Plus, developing creative outlets can also be very valuable to subduing the drama queen syndrome, such as drawing, playing an instrument, working with clay or wood, or writing poetry. So be open-minded, and practice new skills. And remember, you *can* still choose to overreact—but maybe by now you just may not want to.

The Solutions

Differentiating Harmful from Harmless Embellishments

It's fairly safe to assume that most, if not all, people like to be entertained. Being able to laugh, joke around, and poke fun at things in a non-malicious way helps us get rid of stress and feel good. And sometimes telling a story or reporting an event with some extra padding increases entertainment value. However, drama queens sometimes have difficulty knowing when to quit and/or knowing how to turn this process off when dealing with more serious matters. When someone pushes the envelope too far or leads people to believe that the padding is actually part of the quilt, he/she may lose credibility and won't be taken seriously.

So as a general rule of thumb, if you're prone to embellishing, which most drama queens are, then I encourage you to reduce this tendency whenever you are trying to convey a real need to someone. For instance, you'll be taken far more seriously if you were to ask for a hug from your sweetie if you say it like this, "I really had a hard day today. It seemed like everything I tried to do didn't work out the way I expected. I felt disappointed and frustrated. I could really use a hug," as opposed to this, "I thought I was going to die today! Everything got totally screwed up and if you loved me at all you'd see how upset I am and would come and give me some attention." Can you see the difference? Over time, if you communicate your needs and desires as in the second, less desirable, approach you're going to burn people out and probably get rejected a lot. Most people don't want to feel like they are a lifeline to another adult who's supposed to be able to function independently. In the end, you can always save your embellishments for comic relief.

If you're reading this on behalf of a drama queen that you hope to understand better, then I recommend you talk about his or her embellishments by stating clearly, yet gently, that you would be more inspired to listen to her if she were less dramatic in her requests or statements of events. For instance, if your honey gets into her drama queen mode, tell her this: "Gosh, it sounds like you had a tough day. I do love you, but I can't read your mind. I'd be much more receptive to giving you a hug, if you would simply come over and ask for one." Don't get mad, and don't judge. Just state what would help you be more available and keep your boundaries intact.

Next, we're going to tackle *perfectionism*.

Chapter 8

Leaving Perfectionism Behind and Accepting "Good Enough"

Perfectionist ideals often provide the underlying fuel for the over-reactivity commonly displayed by many drama queens. And as a result, drama queens often have trouble coping if they or others perform below the bar they've set. They simply don't have a concept of, or appreciation for, the idea that they can minimize drama and stress by learning to accept "good enough" in areas that truly don't matter in the grand scheme of life. And, by accepting a lesser standard, they would free up a lot more time and energy for attending to the truly significant things in life such as health and well-being, relationships, creativity, and productivity.

Believe me. I know this from firsthand experience. I used to be such a perfectionist in far too many areas of my life. No matter what I was doing or planning it had to be just right—kind of like Goldilocks from the fairy tale, *Goldilocks and the Three Bears*. At times, people literally feared that I would shatter into a million pieces if I erred on the side of being human.

Leaving Perfectionism Behind and Accepting "Good Enough"

I had little tolerance for other people's mistakes as well, but I was the primary recipient of my criticism and perfectionism.

I can recall one time (among many, I may add), when I was throwing a dinner party for a few friends and one of the dishes I made didn't turn out too well. Keep in mind, there were several other dishes that came out great and none of my friends could give a flying **** (you know what) about whether the food was any good or not. All they cared about was having a place to get together and catch up on each other's lives.

Though my friends could care less about my blunder, I couldn't enjoy myself at all because I had made no room in my world for making any mistakes. Mind you, I certainly didn't think I was better than anyone else, or even more capable, I simply lived my life in a state of perpetual fear of losing favor in other people's eyes and of being abandoned. Thus, all I could do was fret about what went wrong with my meatloaf. This just wasn't a way for a college girl to live. I was already doing the best I could with my studies. Did I really need to make such a big deal over a pound of meat that no one else cared about?

Fortunately, although it was a slow process, I eventually pulled myself out of my perfectionism in most areas of my life. In fact, not too long ago I had another party with friends and family and I didn't have enough seats for everyone because I'd miscalculated the number of guests. But, I didn't get all riled up over it. Rather, I simply apologized to the group, shrugged my shoulders, and laughed about it. Then I was able to carry on and have a good time. Granted I had to stand up to eat my dinner, but I looked at it as being able to burn off a few more calories.

Trust me. Breaking free from the perfectionism trap was no easy challenge and it's one in which I need to continually be on top of not to fall back into it. But it's certainly been worth the struggle because life is just far more enjoyable now, with a lot less stress.

If you're someone who believes you need do everything perfectly, I encourage you to pay close attention to the information in this chapter. In order to truly let go and go with the flow, you have to recognize that you simply can't be the best at everything. And even if you *could* be superhuman, you simply don't have enough control over all the other variables in life to be able to make everything turn out just the way you want them to. Nice fairy tale, but not reality.

If you don't believe me, think about this. Imagine trying to get a thousand pound rock to disappear from your backyard. And since it weighs half a ton, you can't possibly move it yourself. *You* may not like where it's parked, but the rock has no feelings and hence it could care less. So to get it to move, you'd probably have to hire a crew and also pay for expensive moving equipment. Hence, you'd have to rely on people to show up as scheduled and do what you request them to do. You can see there are so many variables outside of your control. And even if everyone shows up, they may not do the job as you had envisioned. The point here is that you could work yourself up into a full-fledged drama queen attack if you don't learn to let go of what's outside of your control. And you also have to be able to lighten up on yourself as well.

Now mind you, I'm not suggesting that you lower your perfectionist bar on everything, or even to such a big degree. As I mentioned in the Introduction, you would want to go to a surgeon who was considered a perfectionist in the operating room if you're going under the knife. Makes sense, right? But would you really want this energy thrown at you if you were dating the surgeon and you went to the beach to make sand castles together? Maybe you would, but I'd rather enjoy the feel of the wet sand sliding through my fingers and toes, and watch as the waves knock down my creations now and again. I'd want to be laughing and playing, not making sure every single peak and crevasse of the sand castle met the architectural standards used by civil engineers.

Kyle is a great example of a perfectionist in action. As a web designer and technology guru, Kyle was certainly a master at his trade. People paid him top dollar for his work because they knew they would get their money's worth. But sadly, Kyle could not seem to turn off his perfectionism in other areas of his life. And because of his drama queen syndrome (manifested as a type A personality, extremely high/unrealistic expectations, and a bit of a rage-aholic), when people didn't perform to his standards, he would make a huge deal out of it.

Interestingly Kyle married his wife, Monique, because she was far more mellow than he. And based on his initial attraction, he thought she would be a nice balance in his life. But instead of appreciating her calm demeanor, he became increasingly irritated with her. Monique went about her day with ease and comfort—one of those people drama queens could certainly take a lesson or two from. Mind you, at times she took the idea of living in the moment to a bit of an extreme, in the sense that she often had difficulty making plans ahead of time and sticking to her commitments. She would get easily sidetracked by other things because she was naturally curious about everything. As you can imagine, this would drive someone like Kyle straight to the nuthouse—and I don't mean a place where you'd find cashews and peanuts!

When Kyle and Monique came to couples therapy, Kyle was in for a big surprise. He thought I'd immediately align with his perception that Monique was the problem in their relationship and if only I could fix *her*, he'd calm down. Well, while I certainly did work with Monique on helping her become more organized and less distracted so she could live up to her commitments and not let others down so frequently, this did not help Kyle calm down at all. Okay, there I go again with my own embellishing. Actually Kyle did calm down a bit. But not nearly as much as you'd imagine based on how convincing he'd been stating that Monique's behavior was the source of his stress. Clearly, his drama queen syndrome, specifically his perfectionism, had a history and a life of its own long before he ever met or married Monique.

Initially, Kyle did not like hearing that *his* approach to the world could use some tweaking if he were to ever have the contentment and serenity he claimed to desire. After all, look at how successful he was in his trade. And people clearly reinforced his superior standards by rewarding and praising his fantastic work. But what he didn't realize was that this energy applied in the rest of his life and within his important relationships was costing him plenty with regards to his emotional well-being.

Though he fought me every step of the way, Kyle eventually came around to accept that it wasn't that everyone else in the world was flawed and he was perfect, but that he, too, was a member of the flawed community, just like the rest of us. While he was an expert in his field, he had plenty to learn about how to deal with his emotions and become a better relationship partner. He grew to appreciate the concept that "good enough" is an acceptable standard in most areas of his life. And he also became empowered with the idea that he could *choose* when, where, and with whom he would benefit from raising the bar and when it was best to just leave it at a moderate level. Recognition of this reality was quite eye-opening to Kyle and became the prod that got him to take a look in the mirror and make necessary changes. Boy, was Monique a happy camper after that.

Now, you might be thinking, "Isn't this all the same information as in Chapter Six on changing expectations?" The answer is "no" because even though perfectionism falls within the same arena, it is a particular subset of expectations and worthy of unique attention. It never hurts to hear or read about new information from different angles. Rather, it actually helps strengthen the learning.

Common Underlying Sources Fueling Perfectionism

Perfectionists come in three different packages: (1) those who hold only themselves to an unrealistic standard, (2) those who hold both themselves *and* others to an unrealistic standard, and (3) those who hold only others to an unrealistic standard, expecting everyone else to do things perfectly while letting themselves off the hook. Perfectionists tend to expect flawless performance across the board, from the way someone ties his shoes to how well he is able to meet his own or someone else's needs. However, there can be different levels of perfectionism, with some people becoming uptight about only a handful of things whereas others can't seem to help but put their measuring stick on everything in their lives.

Lots of things can drive a drama queen down the road of perfectionism. Here are a few of the common underlying sources:

- fear of loss of control
- fear of disapproval
- low self-esteem
- fear of loss of love
- critical internalized parent figure pushing for perfectionism
- fear of going unnoticed

The perfectionism serves to camouflage these insecurities and fears. That way, the drama queen, in her perfectionist glory, doesn't have to actually experience these underlying fears. By focusing on perfecting behavior in others and in one's self, the drama queen masks her underlying feelings and creates an illusion of self-worth and of being in control.

Pricilla, a twenty-eight-year-old retail store manager, would explode at her sales staff anytime any one of them didn't perform his duties exactly the way she specified. She had zero tolerance for any individual differences and she held herself to an equally unrealistic standard of perfection. What we later came to realize was that, while other people perceived her as an arrogant bitch, deep down inside she believed that there was nothing special about her and that if she didn't constantly dot all of her i's and cross all of her t's she'd go virtually unnoticed in the world.

Pricilla's perfectionism kept her from feeling this deep-seated fear of inadequacy. And her low self-esteem went unnoticed because she was fixated on what other people were doing wrong. Plus, she was also constantly on her own back to run a perfectly tight ship so that no one would ever see her vulnerabilities.

The Solutions

Pricilla's intimate relationships suffered as well because she could never just sit back and let the day unfold with someone she was involved with. She felt the need to have everything planned out to a tee, with no room for spontaneity. If something didn't go well, she would think it was the end of the world and beat herself up with harsh criticisms and self-attacks. She believed that such behavior toward her own self kept her motivated to perform at such high standards. And she would be highly critical of the people she would date should they make any mistakes at all. Intimate partners quickly lost interest in being her verbal punching bag.

Sadly, Pricilla didn't stay in therapy long enough to understand how her perfectionism was driving people away and actually making her self-esteem even worse. I don't know what happened to her, but I hope she found her way toward making this connection because, even though it was hard to see beneath her tough exterior, she was really a good-hearted and well-meaning young woman. The lesson here is that while perfectionism is meant to serve a valuable purpose in protecting underlying vulnerability, it actually becomes a counter-productive style and does nothing to actually heal the sources of suffering. But once the perfectionist ideal becomes seen as something not so ideal at all, the healing of what's beneath it can actually start to happen.

Now, think for a moment as to what your perfectionism might be covering up. And based on whatever you discover, please vow to make a concerted effort to repair and heal from whatever continues to hurt you within your emotional world.

Accepting Good Enough

For a drama queen who practices perfectionism, the idea of "good enough," especially if used to describe her, can be an image as vile as swallowing a cockroach while sipping a cup of tea. (*Ew!* Now *that's* disgusting.) Perfectionists often don't even know that their bar is set too high. They're so used to their standard that they can't even envision another way. And good enough implies average, which for some drama queens can be a sign of inadequacy or inferiority. Plus, because the need for others' approval is often a very strong underlying motive for the perfectionism, giving up the high standards is perceived as an attack on one's self-worth.

So if you're getting the heebie-jeebies from the concept of average, that's okay for now. Just hear me out and try to apply the tools I recommend. Also, the goal here is to accept "good enough," not necessarily average. You can still be better than average as long as you don't punish yourself or others for making mistakes. But you may need to allow for the average in other people's performance in life, possibly even sub-average. Everyone simply cannot be fantastic at everything. In fact, most people are great at a few things, pretty good at some, average at many, and not very good at some. Perfectionists, however, often deceive themselves into believing they're great at everything or that they should be great at everything. Hence, they often avoid the things they may suck at, thereby missing out on great learning experiences and/or experiences that are fun simply for the sake of being fun.

For instance, take the example of Kyle above. No doubt, Kyle was a truly gifted computer technician. Nevertheless this didn't translate into being a fantastic relationship technician. According to his wife, he was sub-average in being able to have fun and enjoy the moment. He had a really hard time relaxing and just sipping his coffee without being consumed with planning the design of his next project or figuring out a computer glitch. Rather than enjoying the company of his wife (because he didn't have skills in this area), he would go to work leaving himself with very little time on his hands for twiddling his thumbs and/or joining in a fun activity with his wife. But until he got the message that he didn't have to strive to be the most noted computer techie of all time, his inability to be able to enjoy downtime was seriously damaging his relationship with Monique, who wanted a husband she could play with, at least some of the time.

To begin accepting "good enough" in your own life, I'd like you to pick five things you do regularly that range from not good at all to just average (or five things you don't do because of not being very good at them). Then over the course of the next few weeks, try to carve out some time in your day and go down the list and start doing these things. The goal is not to do them in order to get better at them (though this may be a by-product of your efforts). Rather the primary goal is simply to have fun doing them.

Also it's critically important to evaluate how much time and energy you spend searching for approval from others. While it's certainly nice to have the approval from people we care about, oftentimes, people are far too busy with their own lives and problems to pay close enough attention to even notice what you're doing right. As long as you're behaving respectfully to others and taking care of your own responsibilities as an independently functioning adult, it just shouldn't matter so much to you whether other people think you're great. Sure, it's nice to have a few people in your inner circle who think very highly of you, but you just don't need to prove your worthiness all the time to the world at large.

Another exercise you might try is to make a priority list of your life, naming the most important achievements you desire. Try to keep the list to no more than ten items. List them in the order of importance. You can put anything you want on your list. It's your life and so that is for you to decide. You can even have more than ten items on your list. The idea, however, is to find a new balance point in your life. Again, you're reading this to heal from your drama queen syndrome, so something has got to give. But if you're naturally skilled at many things, you may be able to handle more than ten items. Just pay attention to whether your standards get in the way of your peace of mind and emotional well-being. If so, then revise your list and then begin relegating a few to "good-enough" status. *Capiche?*

So please put this concept into effect right away. If you find yourself getting fixated on something that isn't on this list, pause, take a few deep breaths and ask yourself whether this thing you're doing (whatever it is) will really matter to you in a day, a month, a year, or a decade from now. If the answer is "no" then let it go.

The older we get, the faster time seems to fly (even when we're not having fun). So don't waste another minute trying to achieve some perfectionist ideal that doesn't even really exist. When something is really important to you and for your life goals, then give it your all. But if the efforts you assert in an area aren't going to make much of a difference, if any at all, then lighten up and chill out instead.

Chapter 9

Taking Charge of Your Happiness

You're approaching the finish line. Good job! It's not easy looking at your behavior under a magnifying glass and pushing yourself to make changes. But, hopefully the benefits you'll reap will far outweigh the discomfort of your self-scrutiny. Remember, everything you've learned thus far is aimed at helping you become a better batter at life's curve balls and to finally be able to take full charge of your own happiness. And I'm sure by now you're getting the message that life won't always cooperate with your agenda. Hence, it's up to you to learn the best way to handle the ups and the downs so you can ultimately enjoy life to the fullest without getting wigged out by insignificant nuisances.

Ideally, the topics already covered have helped you lay the foundation for your emotional stability and tranquility. But, there are still a few details that will serve as the icing on the cake as we head for the finish line. In this chapter you'll find a potpourri of extra goodies to help you further enhance your ability to lighten up and go with the flow, including learning how to (1) turn chicken shit into chicken salad, (2) live in the moment and reduce anxiety, (3) routinely practice positive self-care,

(4) prevent stress, (5) set good boundaries with yourself and others, and (6) create constructive and creative channels to soothe and subdue the drama queen urges and energy once and for all.

Turning Chicken Shit into Chicken Salad

"Turning chicken shit into chicken salad" is one of my favorite phrases; it may be a little crass, but it usually gets a laugh and lightens up the mood with people who are trying to make positive changes in their lives. Essentially, all this phrase means is turning adversity into strength, or transforming negatives into positives.

I'm going to guess that you haven't perceived your life and your experiences as being all that rosy. You've probably endured your share of hardships, maybe even some trauma. Even if your life has actually been pretty good (though you may have been accused of making mountains out of molehills), it doesn't mean that you haven't suffered real emotional pain. As you now know, it's perception that determines our feelings. So if you have perceived that your life has been hard, it's likely that you have stored painful memories and feelings. Hence, regardless of other people's judgments, you have my empathy for whatever pain and suffering you've experienced. I wish you did not have to endure whatever bad experiences you've lived through or that you didn't interpret your experiences through a dark lens.

But regardless of what I wish for you, it's time for *you* do whatever it takes to put your past behind you. If you carry around unresolved emotional baggage about things that have already happened and are no longer happening now, then your drama queen syndrome will become the least of your worries. Instead, you very well may end up with some serious physical conditions, potentially lethal ones. And you deserve better than that.

So, in order to truly free up your energy to enjoy life today, you must embrace your pain and suffering and give yourself the empathetic acknowledgement you crave. Hence, if you haven't already done so, I want *you* to empathize with your own trials and tribulations and be grateful to have made it through in one piece.

Please note, however, I'm in no way encouraging a pity party. Sitting around and dwelling on what you've been cheated out of in life, or regretting the choices you've made in how to respond to your life's circumstances, will only feed a sense of victimization and will get you nowhere. Rather, simply give yourself some gentle soothing and nurturing for your emotional wounds—that is what the doctor orders! So go on. Put your arms around yourself and squeeze, telling yourself that *you* love and care about yourself, and that, from here onward, you will do the best you can to keep yourself out of harm's way. Please recognize that this is *your* job to do, and no one else's.

Of course, while it's important to approach your history with empathy, that's not all it takes to heal your sensitivities and decrease your tendency to overreact to life. You also have to come to appreciate that whatever you've endured has truly made you stronger. If nothing else, your experiences have given you the capacity for greater compassion and empathy for others. This does not mean that I'm saying it's a good thing that you have suffered or that I hope you continue to have hardships. But hey—as I've repeatedly said, shit happens in life and you need to be able to deal with it and make some chicken salad.

By accepting whatever hardships we've endured, we can then be able to see the positive in all of life's situations. As I've pointed out earlier, I'm certainly not advocating for a Pollyanna view of life. What I am suggesting is that you find the silver lining in even the truly icky experiences. If this is a foreign concept to you or one you've tried to apply in your life but to no avail, please don't give up on it. There are plenty of good resources out in the world to help you heal old baggage. So don't get discouraged. Keep on hunting for whatever help you need to repair and keep on healing. And keep in mind that this journey you're on is about making progress, not achieving perfection.

Taking Charge of Your Happiness

Living in the Moment Anxiety Free

Our bodies experience anxiety the same way we experience fear. However, they are not one and the same. And, the difference between anxiety and fear is a very important one. Whereas fear is the emotion based on real danger, anxiety is the emotion we experience because of *perceived* or *imagined* danger. For instance, if you were to come face-to-face with a mountain lion while you're on a hike, you would naturally feel fear, most likely even a sense of panic. But if you're watching *The Lion King* or observing a den of lions who are caged at the zoo and your body reacts the same as it would in the first scenario, then you're experiencing anxiety.

In order to be able to live in the moment, it's very important to get rid of anxiety. So "how do I do that?" you might be asking. And the answer is: by using the R.E.A.C.T. assessment tool (to assess for real or imagined danger) and then by staying focused on what you actually have control over and letting go of what's out of your control. Again, keep in mind that I'm not messing with any of your body's natural capacities: you can continue to experience fear when there is real danger present and respond appropriately. But I do want to help you eliminate the unnecessary experience of anxiety.

I've alluded to this already, but I want to emphasize again that all you really have control over is your own feelings, thoughts, and behavior. Hence, since these are the things you can control, these are also the same things you can change. But you don't have control over other people's feelings, thoughts or behavior even though they may be influential in how other people feel, think, or behave. You cannot force other people to change. (Granted, the exception to this concept is when you are responsible for a child or another dependent: then you actually can assert some control over his or her behavior, thoughts, and feelings.)

You also have no control over how the world operates at any given moment, whether you're a full-fledged independent adult or still a dependent child. If it's going to rain, then it's going to rain, regardless of your wishful thinking. Or, if a tree outside your house is programmed to dump its leaves at a certain time of year, it's going to do it regardless of whether or not you think the leaves should stay put on the branches because you enjoy their beauty and/or you don't want to have to rake them up.

Drama queens also get notoriously stuck in regretting the past or worrying about the future—two time zones we have absolutely no control over. So at any point when you're dwelling on something that's already happened or on something that you fear will happen in the future, you're weakening your ability to stay centered and present in the immediate moment. That's not to say that you shouldn't spend some of your time contemplating future possibilities and planning ahead. But you do need to stay flexible and appreciate that things outside of your control may upset your agenda.

The message here is to focus your attention on your own life and to not get bogged down by trying to manipulate the aspects of life that are outside of your realm of control. Instead, work hard at being accountable and responsible for your own thoughts, feelings, and behavior. This will give you the best opportunity to achieve the goals you desire. And when unexpected crap falls into your lap, take responsibility for your part and then let go of the rest. For instance, if you're repeatedly late to work because the traffic tends to be very heavy during your commute time each day, stop getting bent out of shape when you encounter traffic. Instead accept that all you can control is your departure time, not how many cars are on the road. Or, if you have legitimate responsibilities that get in your way of leaving on time (like you have to take your mother to dialysis each morning and you can't rearrange her scheduled time), then be proactive and consult with your boss about the possibility of flextime, if that's a reasonable option in your workplace. Communication, from your end, is a great tool that you have full control over. So use it.

Taking Charge of Your Happiness

Practicing Positive Self-Care

Many drama queens go through life often forgetting about the fundamentals of positive self-care. But without a healthy body, we have a lot less stamina to deal with life on a day-to-day basis. In fact, if we don't build in a healthy routine for meeting our basic needs, we can easily become cranky and ill-equipped to handle even the most minor of stressors. How many times have you forgotten to eat a meal or forced yourself to push through your hunger because you were too busy dealing with something else? Or, how often have you forgone a good night's rest because you felt you needed to finish something else you were doing before you allowed yourself to hit the sack, despite barely being able to keep your eyes open? Yet, would you ever put an infant through such deprivation? I should hope not.

While as adults we clearly have more capacity to delay gratification of our needs than do children, drama queens often push the envelope too far, depriving themselves of even basic self-care. Certainly, it's a good thing to be able to postpone gratification when dealing with our preferences or desires, but it's not a good idea to mess with the timing of meeting our body's basic needs. After all, your body is the vehicle with which you experience your life, so it needs proper maintenance and routine care. I know this information may seem entirely elementary or even repetitive. But I can't tell you how often I've encountered people who could write their own handbook on positive self-care, yet they barely practice any of the tips they would include in it.

To assess your level of self-care, I encourage you to rate yourself on the following ten items using the scale below:

never: 0
rarely: 1
sometimes: 2
frequently: 3
always: 4

The Solutions

1. I eat when I'm hungry and stop when I'm full.
2. I eat healthfully.
3. I drink plenty of water daily.
4. I exercise regularly (at least 3-4 times per week with a balance of cardiovascular, strength training, and stretching). (Note: if you have any medical conditions prohibiting any form of exercise, then just skip this question altogether.)
5. I get enough sleep each night, somewhere between six and nine hours or as much as my body needs.
6. I practice good hygiene daily, including teeth care, skin care, hair care, nail care, and care for any other body part requiring attention.
7. I pay attention to my body's basic needs before attending to anything else. (Exception: If you're caring for an infant or other dependent, you may at times need to attend to his/her needs first. So you can still give yourself a 4 if you attend to your needs immediately following the care of a dependent.)
8. I get regular medical check-ups (according to whatever is suggested for my age and family medical history).
9. I maintain a healthy weight according to my age and height.
10. I consciously carve out time each day for attending to my body's needs.

While it would be great to score a 40, this is highly unlikely for most people, even for those who live a relatively stress-free existence. But if you scored anything less than a 30, then you need to pay particular attention to your daily practices of body care. Otherwise you're continuing to give fuel to the drama queen syndrome. So find the areas where you scored a 2 or less and boost these as soon as possible. Then you can work on changing your 3s to 4s whenever you can.

Positive self-care also includes how you attend to your emotional needs. We all have needs for affection, attention, acknowledgement, love, kindness, and respect. And while it's always nice to get our cups filled from other people, it's critically important to be able to fill up our own cups with these goodies, as well. So make sure you don't short-change yourself in this area. Instead, practice embracing these needs and making conscious choices on how to get these met on a daily basis. Be nice to yourself. Talk to yourself with respect and curiosity. Minimize self-criticism and offer yourself inspiration and motivation instead.

Preventing Stress

If only I had a dime for each time I've heard, read, or said to myself how important the art of stress prevention is, I could probably give Oprah a run for her money. Conversely, if I had a dime for each time someone actually followed this advice on a regular basis, I doubt I could even fill up a small piggy bank. That's not because people are inherently lazy or because they don't believe in the value of practicing relaxation methods on a regular basis. Rather, it's because they don't even recognize how stressed they actually are. In fact, countless people, particularly drama queens, are so used to being in high-stress mode, it simply seems normal to them.

As you well know, our society pushes people toward competition and achievement, not to mention racing against the clock. And, while we certainly derive value from climbing the ladder of success (however we each define that) and achieving our goals, the cost for our accomplishments can quickly outweigh the benefits if we don't strike a balance with rest and relaxation. We simply must know how to slow down and appreciate and experience the simple pleasures and aesthetics of life. And, drama queens especially need to learn how to unwind once they've become revved up. But as I've mentioned earlier, stress *management* often fails for drama queens, creating a vicious cycle of more stress and despair.

But before you throw in the towel and think there's no way you'll ever be able to reduce your stress, keep in mind that stress management can certainly be learned. But first, you need to learn stress *prevention*. So don't just nod your head at this advice and do nothing about it. Instead, read on to understand what stress is and then apply the tools on how to minimize its onset.

As you're already aware, just about anything can cause stress, depending upon how a stimulus is perceived. But what you may not know is that even things that are generally described by most people as a stressor ultimately don't have to lead to stress or certainly not to the level or extent you imagine it would. In other words, if you can see the silver lining in the event, then even something that might be upsetting doesn't have to take such a big toll on you. Here are some events that are generally considered stressors (things that produce stress):

- death of a loved one
- illness of oneself or a loved one.
- moving, be it close to or far from your current residence
- getting fired, hired, or changing jobs
- breaking up or entering into a relationship
- the birth of a child
- being a victim of a natural disaster
- getting married
- taking a family vacation

Clearly these don't all have the same weight in terms of how stressful they may be and the degree will change depending upon the particulars of each event. But, in general, if you're free and clear of drama queen thinking and you're grounded as a thriver, then none of these events have to cause overbearing stress. Mind you, that doesn't mean you won't have intense feelings should you encounter any of these situations or feel some level of stress. But, it does mean that you can decide in your own mind whether or not to allow any of these experiences to shatter your world, particularly the ones listed that are generally linked to positive emotions, such as the birth of a child. Sure, there's a lot to be done to prepare for a newborn, and parenting is probably one of the most difficult challenges we face. But the level of stress concerning child care or any other non-emergency event can be significantly reduced by creating a mind set of relaxation and an attitude of "I'll deal with things as they come."

Grant, a middle-aged restaurant owner, had a very hard time handling stress, and he simply refused to make room in his day for relaxation and chillin' out. He was constantly on the go and working himself to the bone. He kept long hours and wouldn't delegate responsibilities to his staff. He felt the need to be hands-on for anything related to his business. His romantic partner, Chad, attempted to be very supportive and understood the demands of Grant's business, but he was growing impatient because he felt like Grant's stresses were dominating their entire lives. Even when they had made decisions together in efforts to create positive changes, Grant was constantly on edge. He didn't get enough sleep and he was wearing himself out with little energy left over for anything else.

When Grant and Chad had put in a bid for a new house (an offer they could clearly afford), Chad thought that Grant's stress would begin to dissipate, since they had been living in a very cramped, too small apartment for four years. So naturally, when Chad shared the news with Grant that their offer had been accepted, Chad expected excitement and celebration. But all Grant could focus on was where the heck he was going to find the time to pack and actually pull off the move.

Much to his own surprise, Chad put his foot down. (Chad tended to be fairly passive and appeasing in the relationship.) Basically, Chad gave Grant the ultimatum that if he didn't learn how to balance his life, he was going to move on to a relationship that would bring him more joy. Thankfully, Grant got the message that he needed to start working on de-stressing and participating in his entire life, not just his restaurant business.

So don't wait until a loved one threatens to leave you or a doctor tells you you're going to have a coronary if you don't slow down. Instead recognize that life has many facets and you should be participating fully in as many as you can and with as little stress as possible.

Below is a list of tips to keep your stress level to a minimum. I recommend you practice at least two or three of these each day. Mix them up and do different ones at different times paying close attention to which ones provide the best results for you. Also, don't stop at the suggestions on my list, get creative and come up with your own ideas. (Please note a few of these were already included in positive self-care. Naturally, there would be some overlap between self-care and minimizing stress.)

1. Practice all the items on the positive self-care assessment tool. A healthy body will help yield a healthy mind.

2. Keep a daily journal of the things that you allowed to bug you that day and then consciously release the negative feelings by acknowledging that "this too shall pass." Over time, re-check earlier entries to keep track of your progress.

3. Engage in play therapy. Do you ever notice how much fun a child can have with a couple of pots and pans and some wooden spoons, or with a bucket, shovel, and a sandbox? Well, you don't have to be a kid to enjoy the art of playing. Get out there and do the activities that give you peace of mind and fully enjoy them while you're engaged in them. (I recently rediscovered the hula hoop. I used to be able to swirl one of those hoops around my body for hours and hours without a care in the world. Granted, I'm clearly not in the same shape as I was as a young teen, but it sure is fun to give it a whirl for as long as my belly muscles can take it. Plus, it's just great to feel like a carefree kid again!)

4. Cuddle. You don't need to have a significant other in your life to get cuddles. Trusted friends or close family members can be good sources of TLC, as can pets. Plus, while certainly not a replacement for human contact, in a pinch you might even try squeezing a stuffed animal or a cushy pillow. And believe it or not, even *you* can

be a source for your own cuddles. Put your arms around your body and give yourself a nice big squeeze. Self-induced hugs can be very gratifying once you get over the idea that hugs are only meaningful when they come from other people. Try it. You might like it.

5. Stimulate all of your senses. Light candles, add new herbs and spices to your food, listen to a variety of music, visit beautiful places and soak in the scenario. When we tantalize our senses with pleasurable sounds, scents, and sights, we create an environment in our bodies that is mutually exclusive to a state of stress.

6. Have a few, short, pep talks with yourself each day using positive affirmations. And regularly give yourself a pat on the back for making efforts toward increased physical, emotional, and mental well-being.

7. Breathe, breathe, and breathe some more. I recommend you practice deep breathing exercises at least three times per day, everyday, for the rest of your life. No kidding. Why? Because stress and relaxation are two mutually exclusive events. You simply can't be stressed out and calm at the same moment. And the quickest and easiest way to induce relaxation is through increased oxygen intake. This doesn't have to be a long, drawn out process. Just spend a few minutes with your eyes closed, breathing in through your nose (unless you're stuffed up, then your mouth will do just fine), and exhaling through your mouth. When you have extra time, you can practice a more focused and lengthy relaxation method of tensing and loosening the muscles in your body, starting with your toes and working your way up all the way to the top of your head—all the while continuing to deep breathe. (Note: don't continue if you start hyperventilating or getting dizzy as you could actually make things worse.)

8. Improve your time management. Balancing commitments and organizing our lives is critical to preventing stress, particularly for high-level drama queens. While we've clearly established that life

can certainly disrupt our plan of action, this reality creates even more stress and drama if we fail to at least take charge of managing our time efficiently. The key to managing our time well requires setting priorities and avoiding the trap of procrastination. Basically, if you routinely put too many items on your "to-do list" and/or you allow yourself to get distracted by things that aren't a priority, you're bound to get overwhelmed and then become even more vulnerable to wigging out over trivial matters. And if you put things off for another time when you could be completing a task or a goal in the present moment, then when life hits you with something you didn't anticipate, you'll be racing against the clock, leaving yourself wide open for stress and over-reactivity. So get on top of your schedule and take charge of what you can.

9. Laugh out loud. I mean it. Laughter helps us unwind and de-stress, even when something seems very serious. So, unless you're faced with a life or death situation or some other urgent matter, you can probably find the humor in it. Should you find yourself getting revved up over nonsense, then go see a funny movie, visit a comedy club, or read a silly joke book. Personally, I love watching shows about animals doing goofy things—that really helps me loosen up. But you need to find something that tickles your sense of humor.

10. Practice meditation. I know this is a very new-age recommendation, but hey, people from all over the world have been telling us the benefits of this practice for our body, mind, and spirit. This doesn't have to be some deeply intense, time-consuming exercise. Rather, just get your hands on a CD that talks you through a meditation or even a self-hypnosis CD aimed at stress reduction and relaxation.

Taking Charge of Your Happiness

Setting Good Boundaries

Let's face it. People make unreasonable requests all the time. I know I have been guilty of doing so and I'm pretty sure you have, too. But being faced with an unreasonable request, whether from a loved one, child, coworker, family member, or even a stranger, doesn't have to activate the queen in you. Why? Because a request isn't a demand. And even if someone makes a demand on you, you can still say *"no"* (unless of course someone has taken away your power—but let's hope that's never the case). The reverse is also true: people also have the right to say "no" to you.

Being able to maintain healthy boundaries often means reevaluating your relationships with others. Sadly, many people do try to cross over the lines we draw and don't respect our rights. When this is the case, particularly with people who repeatedly devalue our limits, it's time to seriously consider ending these relationships. Keeping toxic people in your life will inevitably re-ignite the drama queen syndrome. As a friend of mine once said, "You can only be functional in a dysfunctional situation for so long; the dysfunction will inevitable rule." Hence, remember that while you don't have control over how other people act, you clearly have choices about what you will or won't tolerate in your relationships.

Sometimes we may choose to cut certain people a bit of slack, even if they're not the healthiest of individuals. For instance, you may tolerate your grandmother's critical demeanor because she is older and perhaps not as strong as you, and she doesn't have any control over your life and your choices anyway. But I wouldn't suggest you have her come live with you, unless you have developed a very thick skin and can shield yourself completely from her attitude. Or, you may tolerate a difficult boss because you're learning invaluable skills at your job and you don't have to interact with that person all that much. And if you have good "shake off" skills—you can easily let her personality roll off of your back and not let his/her undesirable behavior get under your skin. Clearly, if your job requires frequent, prolonged interaction with a difficult boss, it may be better to consider finding another job. But even in these situations, you'd be surprised how much you might be able to ignore, once you're able to detach and set boundaries.

But some people we keep in our lives really should get booted out. In fact, if you want to stay on track with your mental health-seeking mission, you may need to dump a friendship or romantic relationship if the friend or lover repeatedly disregards your needs and violates your space. I don't suggest you do this hastily, as you don't want to react on impulse. But, concerning some people (such as those emotional vampire types), you should truly give thought and consideration to whether there's really any benefit at all to these relationships, and then become willing to make adjustments should you discover toxic patterns. While we need other people in our lives, we don't need any one particular person and certainly not anyone who mistreats us.

So go through all of your significant relationships and do a cost-benefit analysis. For those who have overstayed their welcome and aren't interested in growing along with you, it's time to move them out of your inner circle and make room for those who will treat you with the love and respect you deserve.

Mind you, it is as important to set and maintain healthy boundaries with ourselves as well as it is with others. Sometimes you have to say "no" to yourself because the long-term consequences of giving in to your own requests often far outweigh any short-term gains. For instance, you may really want to go out on the town on Saturday night and blow off steam with your friends. But if you've had a really tough week at work, or have been in a fight with your significant other for the past few days and you've lost sleep, then it probably wouldn't be a good idea to run yourself ragged over the weekend. Instead you might have to renegotiate with yourself, making a deal to get the rest you need this week and then plan a night out for the following Saturday.

Taking Charge of Your Happiness

Note: to significant others of a drama queen: you might be reading this and thinking, "Why do I keep hanging in there with this drama queen? Maybe I should just cut my losses and move on?" Well, of course I can't tell you to stay in a relationship that's been difficult if you're already fed up. But I would suggest that you might consider giving the relationship a bit more time, especially if you're connected to a lovable drama queen who is willing to actually make the changes recommended in this book. You may end-up being the recipient of some very big benefits.

Channeling the Drama Queen Energy through Creativity and the Performing Arts

While you may have zero interest in pursuing creative outlets through the performing arts, don't knock it until you've at least given it some thought. Remember, drama queen energy can be very entertaining and creative. In fact, if you're not already in the performing arts or participating in a creative endeavor, you may have missed your calling. Beneath your over-reactivity lie beautiful qualities like sensitivity and compassion. Sadly, these qualities often stay dormant because the over-reactivity has commanded all of your attention, not to mention the attention of others around you. However, once channeled in the right places and at the right times, aspects of your drama queen style can become your greatest gift. Hey, society loves to watch a brilliantly talented drama queen on the big screen or onstage. We applaud such intensity and flair.

Vanessa, a business major at a popular university, felt as though she had to pursue a career in accounting to win her parents' approval. Even though she had proven herself to be a very talented singer and actress during her high school years, her parents thought she should have a "stable" career. So Vanessa, being the dutiful daughter, chucked her dreams of stardom and went on to learn how to crunch numbers. Mind you, there's nothing wrong with a career in accounting, if that's what you're suited for. But for Vanessa, turning her back on her talents was akin to a death sentence.

By her third year in college, Vanessa had become incredibly impatient and unmotivated and she moved from a low-level drama queen to a high level one. Whereas in the past she'd show tendencies to overreact to minor disruptions, now she found herself erupting in despair and agitation for no apparent reason at all. She just couldn't put her finger on what was bugging her so much. Well, as it turns out, Vanessa no longer had any creative outlets for her pent-up emotional energy.

Of course, Vanessa had many things to learn to be able to subdue the drama queen in her, but of greatest value to her was learning that she really didn't have to give up her dreams at all. And it was music to her ears to have me suggest to her that she get back involved in the creative arts. Vanessa found an acting workshop and joined immediately. And she found a few establishments that offered amateur singing nights where she could belt out a few chords now and again. Though she continued to finish her degree so that she could have a fall-back position, she felt far more hopeful about her future. Who knows? Maybe someday she'll make it to the big screen after all.

If you're not already in the performing arts or involved in a creative endeavor, you could try any number of outlets, including writing, acting workshops, small theater, stand-up comedy, art, photography, or learning to play a musical instrument. Who knows what kind of talent you may have buried beneath the surface. Hey, if the secret be told: I didn't pursue my writing and TV work solely because I wanted to be able to help more people than I can reach within a private practice or clinic setting. I wish I were that altruistic, but I'm not. Remember, I too am a recovering drama queen, just like you!

If you don't believe that you're cut out for any of these outlets, you can direct your drama queen energy through all sorts of other creative channels. You could take up cooking, sewing, pottery making, or woodworking. You could plant an exotic flower garden or get involved in a political campaign where your passion and enthusiasm would yield tremendous positive energy. Just get out there and put your energy into something that will flourish.

Also, if you're the type of drama queen who loves a good adrenaline rush, then you're going to need some new outlets for creating positive excitement. Let's face it. Some folks really get off on high-risk activities and they just won't be happy with a tranquil life all of the time. As long as you're not adding stress and/or taking risks that could seriously harm you, then go ahead and enjoy the things that give you the rush. There are loads of activities you could try, from skydiving (as long as you have a parachute) to hiking Mt. Whitney. You might enjoy downhill skiing, car-racing, or galloping on a horse through an open field. As long as you get the training you need to participate safely, you can do anything you wish. And because you will be consciously and purposefully *choosing* these activities, you won't be reinstating your drama queen syndrome. So, knock yourself out and have some exciting adventures, if these appeal to you!

Chapter 10

When Self-Help Isn't Enough

By no fault of your own, sometimes self-help simply won't provide the relief you desire. You may have read through the chapters and practiced all the tools and tips throughout the book, but you still find yourself overreacting to the common day-to-day ups and downs. If this describes you, please don't give up hope. It's possible that you (or your loved one) suffer from one or more of the many psychological conditions that will inevitably interfere with your ability to derive much benefit from the information and recommendations included in this book. Our discussion would not be complete without at least mentioning the other common conditions that may lie at the heart of the drama queen syndrome. While there are certainly other disorders that resemble the drama queen syndrome, the one I believe to have the most overlap include borderline and hysterical personality disorder, post-traumatic stress disorder, anxiety disorder, and bipolar disorder.

As you read on, please keep in mind that the good news is that these conditions are treatable, but they should not be ignored. You may require professional help, including medication assessment and/or psycho-therapy.

The descriptions below are summarized and paraphrased from the *Diagnostic and Statistical Manual of Mental Disorders—Fourth Edition Text Revision*, American Psychiatric Association, 2000. Please keep in mind that you should not attempt to diagnose yourself; proper diagnosis requires a trained professional who has years of experience distinguishing among the various disorders. Also, it's common for people to read a description of a disorder and distort it to fit their own agendas. (If you want something to be the answer to your suffering, you'll likely only notice the items that describe you.) Conversely, if you don't want something to fit, then you'll likely only see the pieces that rule you out. People just aren't able to be as objective as they might like to believe they can be, especially when it comes to diagnosing their own ailments.

Please also keep in mind that I've not listed these conditions in any order of severity. In fact, within each category there is a range in severity from mildly disruptive to severely disruptive to one's life in terms of social, occupational, and emotional well-being. So don't pass judgment or fall into a shame hole if you see your reflection in one or more of these descriptions. Would you judge or berate yourself if you developed symptoms of tiredness, weight gain, appetite increase, and then discovered you suffer from anemia or a thyroid condition? I would *hope* not. Rather, most likely you'd seek the recommended medical treatment and get on your way back to physical well-being. So, this should be no different when dealing with your mental health.

The following descriptions provide an overview or synopsis of what you might be dealing with, not comprehensive information. So please review the following descriptions from the viewpoint of being curious to discover other *possible* explanations for your particular drama queen syndrome (or that of your significant other). If one or more of these descriptions reflects your experience of your symptoms, please seek further assistance. You can try researching these conditions further on the Internet, but don't stop there. Seek professional help, using the resources available in your community.

Personality Disorders

You may or may not have ever heard of what's known as a *personality disorder*. And, quite frankly, I don't care much for this label, since people tend to believe this term implies that someone has a "bad" personality. And that is far from the truth. People with personality disorders may be extremely likeable and function quite well. Thus, rather than thinking of this category as having anything to do with the quality of one's personality, it's better to think of it as referring to whether or not one has flexibility in style with regards to responding to the world. People with personality disorders tend to have an inflexible style: that is, they react to and perceive the world in virtually the same fashion regardless of the changing scenarios.

For instance, someone who suffers from *paranoid personality disorder* operates in the world with a tendency toward suspecting people of malevolent motives—that is, suspecting that people are out to harm her or of trying to pull the wool over her eyes. She'll have trouble trusting anyone and will likely interpret any situation where something doesn't seem quite right as evidence that people are trying to exploit or deceive her. This is not situational as in the case of someone who is actually being stalked, nor is it a transient condition as in the case of someone who suffers from schizophrenia, paranoid type, which does not fall under the classification of a personality disorder but is, rather, a psychotic disorder. This may seem confusing, but hang in there with me, as I think the picture will get clearer. Someone with *paranoid personality disorder* pretty much operates the same way day in and day out. She's not in an acute phase of a psychotic breakdown with hallucinations and persecutory delusions. Rather, this is just how she operates in the world. Even with people with whom she develops close relationships, she's bound to continually be suspicious of their intentions and be likely to continually misinterpret their behavior.

At this point within the field of psychology and psychiatry, ten different personality disorders have been identified. Someone may suffer from a combination of two or more. Or he/she may not meet the full criteria of a personality disorder, yet have what's known as "features" of the particular type. Personality disorders are not to be confused with personality traits, which we all have. Personality traits are also enduring patterns of responding to a variety of social and personal contexts, but they have much more flexibility.

Despite the differences in personality disorders, there are overlapping characteristics to them all. According to the *Diagnostic And Statistical Manual of Mental Disorders*, "a personality disorder is an enduring pattern of inner experience and behavior that deviates markedly from the expectations of the individuals culture, is pervasive and inflexible, has an onset in adolescence or early adulthood, is stable over time, and leads to distress or impairment."* Basically, if one meets the criteria for a personality disorder, then by and large, this implies that the person has a more rigid style of coping with life and of responding to it. This inflexibility can be seen in all contexts of one's life, including social relationships, personal relationships, and occupational functioning. In essence, regardless of the situation and stimuli, the person reacts similarly and predictably. Hence people who suffer from personality disorders have great difficulty modifying their behavior. It's common for people with these disorders to blame others for their unhappiness or distress and to perceive themselves as victims regardless of the situation.

---

*Reprinted with permission from the licensing manager for the American Psychiatric Publishing—verbally granted on March 28, 2008, from Chad Thompson.

The Solutions

People with a personality disorder aren't trying to annoy others. They're usually completely unaware that they even have a disorder at all. When they're bothered by things, they tend to see the source as something outside themselves, often having difficulty believing that they have the power to change anything. They may be very loving, kind, and highly ethical, but they simply can't seem to help themselves from responding in their characteristic style. They certainly can be happy individuals and many people they might encounter in their lives wouldn't even know that they suffer from a clinically diagnosable condition. But because they tend to be so rigid, other people often have a hard time getting along with them and their relationships tend to suffer as a result.

The two personality disorders that most closely resemble the drama queen syndrome are *borderline personality disorder* (BPD) and *histrionic personality disorder* (HPD). Both of these are characterized by attention-seeking behavior in order to gain the concern of others. However, unlike people with some other personality disorders (like *narcissistic personality disorder*), the goal of the attention-seeking behavior is not to exploit others or gain power, but rather to command the *concern* of others because they are plagued by feelings of loneliness and emptiness.

BPD is characterized by impulsive behavior, unstable self-image, and problems in interpersonal relationships. It often comes along with several of the following features: persistent efforts to keep from being abandoned or rejected, self-destructive behavior (may include anything from self-mutilation to bulimia to substance abuse to suicidal gestures or attempts), extreme mood fluctuations (often as a result of feeling slighted by someone in a relational context), rageful outbursts, and severe feelings of emptiness.

The primary features of HPD is high emotionality and attention-seeking behavior that is persistent across time and context and is often associated with inappropriate sexually seductive behavior, superficial or rapidly shifting emotions, a heavy focus on physical appearance to draw attention to oneself, highly dramatic, and suggestible. People with HPD often perceive the relationships they cultivate to be far more intimate than they actually are. As you read this description of HPD, you'll probably be very tempted to jump to the conclusion that you or your loved one who suffers from the drama queen syndrome has this personality disorder. And you might be right, but please keep in mind that meeting the requirement for a personality disorder requires a steady and pervasive response pattern that is inflexible to change. Also, these behaviors are very intense and not just occasionally beyond the norm. So don't rule it out, but be careful not to jump to premature conclusions. All these descriptions must be put into a context that includes cultural and familial standards and norms.

Posttraumatic Stress Disorder

The most important feature of *posttraumatic stress disorder* (PTSD) is that the symptoms develop as a direct result of witnessing or being part of an extremely traumatic event outside the realm of normal human experience where an individual experienced extreme feelings of horror, helplessness, or terror. Plus, to warrant this diagnosis, the characteristic features must not have been present before experiencing the disturbing event. Some examples of traumatic events include: being held up at gunpoint, being the driver of or passenger in a near-fatal car crash, witnessing a loved one jump to his death from a ten-story building, being kidnapped or raped, or finding out that your child has suddenly died. The symptoms that follow from the trauma last for at least a month or longer and include: a reexperiencing of the traumatic event (such as recurring imagery, nightmares, flashbacks) often accompanied by intense physiological reactions, as though the trauma is happening all over again in the moment, deliberate avoidance of anything that reminds the person of the event or triggers the memory of the traumatic event (such as avoiding all images of war if someone lost a son during a military engagement), hypervigilance to danger, and difficulty sleeping and/or concentrating. Some people with PTSD become very irritable, demonstrating outburst of anger and overreactivity. Others report feeling very detached from others and pessimistic about the future.

PTSD can range from mild to severe. Some people with PTSD become very adept at controlling their environment so as to avoid re-encountering any triggers that might activate unwanted arousal and/or intrusive memories of the trauma. Of course, they can be a ticking time bomb when faced with unexpected situations where their control is limited. Their reactions may be very alarming to others around them because the traumatic triggers aren't visible to others and they won't have the same associations. For instance, a woman who has been raped may be driving on the street one day and see a billboard advertisement for an upcoming movie that depicts a man stalking a woman. If she suffers from PTSD, she might begin hyperventilating because the image triggers her memory of her trauma. Someone without PTSD might see the same billboard and have no visceral response at all. PTSD can also result from repeated and chronic exposure to abuse or threats of abandonment during childhood.

Left untreated, PTSD can seriously debilitate someone's life. Again, don't jump to premature conclusions, but if this description for PTSD reflects your experience, please seek professional help so that you can free yourself from the painful recurring memories, intrusive thoughts, and resulting over-reactive and avoidant behavior. You deserve to have your world re-open to all the wonderful possibilities of living.

Anxiety Disorder

If you recall, one of the dominant features often that prompts a drama queen reaction is a tendency to worry about things that haven't yet happened and fearing the worst outcome. This description also characterizes people who suffer from *generalized anxiety disorder* (GAD). But in order to be diagnosed with GAD, several other features need to be present as well. The criteria for GAD include: having excessive anxiety or worry most of the time for a minimum of 6 months (not a fleeting moment of anxiety that is situationally induced, as in someone who's about to parachute from an airplane for the first time), unable to control the worry, restlessness, difficulty concentrating, problems falling or staying asleep, irritability, and getting tired easily. Some people with GAD also have severe, ongoing muscle tension and can't seem to relax. And, these symptoms cause either *impairment* in one's functioning or severe subjective *distress*.

There also exist many medical conditions that may be the cause of the anxiety symptoms (such as hyperthyroidism, chronic obstructive pulmonary disease, or vitamin deficiencies). Plus certain medications and substances may also be associated with anxiety as a side effect. All of these possibilities need to be ruled out if your dominant symptom is anxiety. Again, the information here is insufficient to yield a diagnosis. You'll need a professional assessment and evaluation. You should not have to live in a perpetual state of worry. There is help available, so take action now.

Bipolar Disorder

Bipolar disorder is a subcategory of mood disorders wherein the disturbance of mood is the prominent characteristic. The category of bipolar disorder includes three types: *bipolar I, bipolar II*, and *cyclothymic disorder*. I know this is a bit confusing if you're not familiar with these terms. But essentially, to meet the criteria for bipolar I, you must have had at least one manic episode and may or may not have ever had a major depressive episode. To meet the criteria for bipolar II, you must have had at least one depressive episode and at least one hypomanic episode. A diagnosis of cyclothymic disorder requires at least two years of experiencing a mixture of hypomania and depressive symptoms, but is not severe enough to meet the criteria for major depressive disorder.

The Solutions

For the purpose of this section, however, I just want you to get a sense for the fact that what looks like the drama queen syndrome could actually be a far more serious condition, requiring medical and psychotherapeutic intervention.

Many people have complained of feeling down or depressed sometime in their lives. And many people would also report having had periods where they've felt on top of the world. But, these experiences don't qualify as clinically diagnosable conditions of major depressive disorder or manic/hypomanic episodes. But for simplicity sake, you can picture these on a continuum from severe depression (including suicidal thoughts and attempts) to extreme elation and grandiosity (including delusions of grandeur).

Most people vacillate somewhere in the middle, possibly moving a degree or two from the center. Drama queens move around a bit more. But those who suffer bipolar disorder have often lived their lives on the two extreme ends, sometimes with one end more dominant than the other.

A major depressive episode involves the presence, for a minimum of two consecutive weeks, of depressed mood and/or loss of interest or pleasure in the things or people in life that you usually enjoy. Depression is also accompanied by at least a few of the following: significant weight loss or changes in appetite, trouble sleeping or sleeping too much, lack of energy, agitation or a slowing down in movements as observed by others, feelings of worthlessness, excessive guilt, difficulty concentrating, and/or thoughts of suicide. These symptoms cause severe distress and/or affect one's ability to function. If these symptoms are caused by the loss of a loved one, they do not constitute a major depressive episode, but would be better described as *bereavement*.

A manic episode is characterized by at least one week of a persistently elevated, euphoric, or irritable mood, causing severe disturbance in occupational or social functioning, accompanied by: grandiosity (believing oneself to be better than anyone else), inability to sleep (and not wanting to), excessive talkativeness, racing thoughts that don't often make any sense, high distractibility, hyper focus on a goal, and excessive indulgence in pleasure-inducing activities (shopping sprees, sexual promiscuity, impulsive business decisions). A relatively conservative person who would never dream of engaging in high-risk behavior, might hop on a plane and run off to a happening city, leaving his family behind without any notice, while in the midst of a manic episode. And if you tell him he's being irresponsible, he might flip you off and tell you where to go, letting you know in no uncertain terms that anything you have to say doesn't matter to him at all. Seeing someone you love in the midst of a manic episode can be very alarming and frightening, almost like a Dr. Jekyll and Mr. Hyde story. It's not a pretty sight. And often, after coming out of the episode, the person may feel very embarrassed when reminded of his behavior. To understand what a hypomanic episode is, just think of it as having very similar features to a manic episode, but less intense.

Many drama queens may report feelings and symptoms as intense as those present in a depressive or manic episode, but often these are an exaggeration. But, nevertheless, these feelings should not be taken lightly. If you believe you fit into these categories, then please get an evaluation.

As mentioned previously, all of these conditions are treatable. Some people require medication, but often, depending upon the person, his history, and the intensity of the disorder, psychotherapy may be sufficient. There are many forms of psychotherapy, and treatment should be adapted to meet your particular needs.

Seeking Professional Help

Seeking help can often become an overwhelming process. It's hard to how to know what kind of help you need, from whom, and where to find it. Plus, many people don't have good health-care coverage and many insurance companies don't provide any coverage for mental health at all. Combine that with the fact that most people don't have unlimited financial resources to spend on doctors and specialists and low-cost health care is very hard to find, and we have a recipe for people not being able to get the assistance they often need. Tragic, but true. So—what to do?

While resources may be hard to find, don't give up hope. Unless you live in an extremely rural town, far out of reach from health care facilities, you should be able to find organizations and community services somewhere within your area. You just need to be persistent and dedicated to your cause.

Should you believe that you are in need of extra assistance, and you're doing a blind search, here are some suggestions:

1. If you have mental health-care coverage that you plan to use, contact your insurance company and ask for a list of providers who are covered under your plan.

2. If you don't have insurance coverage and your budget won't allow for more than a nominal fee, if anything, contact the local free or low-cost clinics in your area. You can also contact local hospitals or residential treatment centers to find out about getting financial aid. Some hospitals have research programs where they conduct clinical trials to evaluate the effectiveness of new medications and treatments. If you qualify, you might be able to get the latest treatments at no cost to you.

3. If you or someone you love suffers from mental illness, you may be able to qualify for state disability. You can find out more about this process at http://www.ssa.gov/pubs/10029.html.

4. If you have a trusted friend or family member who has undergone treatment, you might consider asking him or her for a referral. Or you could ask your physician.

5. The Internet can be extremely helpful in helping you search for resources in your area. If you don't have online access, you can always

go to your local public library and use the Internet. Two valuable online resources include: National Mental Health Association at http://www.nmha.org/ and National Alliance on Mental Illness at http://www.nami.org/

6. Please be careful and screen any referrals you find. Make sure the person is qualified and licensed to practice psychotherapy, such as psychologists, licensed marriage and family therapists, or licensed clinical social workers. If you're considering medication, you should get an evaluation from a psychiatrist. You should also get a full physical exam to rule out any underlying medical conditions that could be causing your symptoms.

Now, sit back for a moment and give yourself a big hug. You have taken a really big step toward improving your overall mental and emotional well-being simply by reading this book. Plus, if you actually practice and put to use the tools recommended, you should continue to see progress and further gains. And, if you've discovered that you need more than this self-help tool, then I trust you will make it a priority to find the support you need.

Three cheers for you!

One Final Note to Significant Others

The fact that you would bother to read this book on behalf of your loved one shows how much you must care about your lovable drama queen. But, please keep in mind that no matter how much you may love or care for someone who is struggling with a syndrome or disorder, you can only do so much. You can be sensitive, compassionate, and understanding. But you have needs too, and it's important that you take good care of yourself and don't allow someone else's issues dominate your life.

You can communicate your care and concern and offer to be of help, but you can't force someone to deal with his or her issues if she's unwilling. So don't beat yourself up if you have made many attempts to help your significant other but have gotten nowhere. Sometimes you may just have to let go and move on. But, hopefully, the information within these pages has given you food for thought and some new ways to think about your lovable queen. And, maybe you'll be able to plant a seed of recovery so that your loved one will get the help she or he needs!

Index

Index

Index

Index